Cry on Desert Winds

Also by Bea Carlton
in Large Print:

Deadly Gypsy Blue
In the Foxes' Lair
In the House of the Enemy
Moonshell
The Secret of Windthorn
Terror in the Night
Touch of the Black Widow
Voices from the Mist
Where's Jessie?

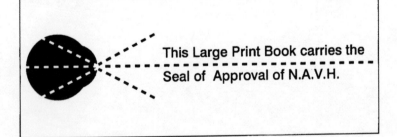

This Large Print Book carries the
Seal of Approval of N.A.V.H.

Cry on Desert Winds

BEA CARLTON

Thorndike Press • Waterville, Maine

Copyright © 1991 Accent Publications
Sequel to Touch of the Black Widow

Published in 2004 by arrangement with Bea Carlton.

Thorndike Press® Large Print Christian Mystery.

The tree indicium is a trademark of Thorndike Press.

The text of this Large Print edition is unabridged.
Other aspects of the book may vary from the original edition.

Set in 16 pt. Plantin by Christina S. Huff.

Printed in the United States on permanent paper.

Library of Congress Cataloging-in-Publication Data

Carlton, Bea.
    Cry on desert winds / Bea Carlton.
      p. cm.
    Sequel to: Touch of the black widow.
    ISBN 0-7862-5709-1 (lg. print : hc : alk. paper)
    1. Arizona — Fiction. 2. Mansions — Fiction.
  3. Criminals — Fiction. 4. Large type books. I. Title.
PS3553.A736C78 2004
813′.54—dc21
                                       2003053353

Dedicated with much love
to our newest daughter and grandson,
Gayle and Nathan.

As the Founder/CEO of NAVH, the only national health agency solely devoted to those who, although not totally blind, have an eye disease which could lead to serious visual impairment, I am pleased to recognize Thorndike Press* as one of the leading publishers in the large print field.

Founded in 1954 in San Francisco to prepare large print textbooks for partially seeing children, NAVH became the pioneer and standard setting agency in the preparation of large type.

Today, those publishers who meet our standards carry the prestigious "Seal of Approval" indicating high quality large print. We are delighted that Thorndike Press is one of the publishers whose titles meet these standards. We are also pleased to recognize the significant contribution Thorndike Press is making in this important and growing field.

Lorraine H. Marchi, L.H.D.
Founder/CEO
NAVH

* Thorndike Press encompasses the following imprints: Thorndike, Wheeler, Walker and Large Print Press.

1

The stumbling figure was dwarfed by the immensity of the hot, empty desert sands, cactus, and rocks as she staggered forward on blistered, tortured feet. She reeled against sharp-thorned palo verde and scarcely felt the pain. A lone buzzard circled high overhead, its cold eyes fixed upon the girl.

She stopped for a moment, tottering on her feet, then pitched forward on her face. The buzzard began a spiraling descent toward the fallen figure. Another of the grisly carrion birds, red head and black body glistening in the sun, rose on heavy flapping wings from a perch on a leaning, ancient wood post and came to rest on the ground a few yards away from the fallen girl.

The panting figure moved slightly and raised her head to stare with blurred eyes at the large bird. Horror dawned slowly in the heat-dazed mind. Struggling weakly, the girl managed to draw herself to a sitting position.

"Conchita," she whispered hoarsely.

Placing her hands on the blistering earth, she slowly came to her feet, swaying under the burning, merciless sun. The buzzard flapped back to the post and settled on it. The other buzzard landed on a nearby boulder, hopping about nervously but keeping a close watch on the girl.

"I'm-so-hot." The words whispered in Spanish through parched lips. Her tongue felt as dry as the sand under her sandaled feet and too big for her mouth. She felt locked in a furnace from which there was no relief.

She looked up. A small pond! She lurched toward it for a few yards, then cried out as it vanished and only sand and rocks, cactus and strong-scented creosote bushes remained. Sobbing with tears she didn't know her parched body had, she sank to her knees but rose again as the sand burned through her coarse cotton skirt like a hot stove grate.

Nothing moved, except the cold eyes of the two — now motionless — buzzards. Even the lizards and horned toads had sought relief from the relentless heat under rocks and in abandoned rabbit holes.

If only I can go on, maybe there will be water somewhere. The thought filled her mind. She forced herself to move one foot a short step and then the other.

A rolling sound forced away the thoughts of scorching sand and searing thirst. Thunder! She shaded her eyes with an unsteady hand. Yes! Far to the west a dark cloud was forming. A hot wind laden with stinging sand suddenly swirled about her, and she covered her face with shaking hands to shield her burning eyes.

Her heart began to pound. "Dear God," she whispered, "please let it rain on me." She turned and staggered toward the rapidly building clouds.

Suddenly, above the far-off thunder and the whine of the rising desert winds, there came a new sound. A vehicle! Terror possessed her. Were they coming back to see if anyone was left alive?

With a strangled cry, she tried to run. Now she could see the dust from the vehicle and hear the growl of the engine as it moved up a small hill. Throwing herself into a small eroded gully, she crawled as far as she could under the thin foliage of a low palo verde tree.

Her breath was coming in gasps now and violent pain gripped her head. She curled up, trying to bury her head in her rough skirt to shut out the intense, burning light from the sun above. Frightened sobs tore at her parched throat. She gripped her mouth to keep from crying out. Then, the world whirled about her, and darkness came swiftly down upon her.

The Jeep rolled by, sending up clouds of powdery dust. But Luana did not see it or the hawk-eyed gaze of its driver as it moved slowly over the seared landscape, probing . . . searching. Nor did she feel the sudden spatter of raindrops on her fevered face. She lay as still as death.

2

Driving rain and violent wind gusts pounded the Windthorn station wagon as it crept down the Organ Pipe Cactus National Monument road toward Why, Arizona.

Skye Windthorn's lean form hunched over the wheel, slate-grey eyes straining to glimpse the white center line through the streaming rain. The rapidly moving windshield wipers seemed to have little effect on the blinding sheets of water.

A streak of lightning illuminated the interior of the car briefly and the blonde-headed girl in the back seat jumped, squealing in alarm. On the other end of the seat, a slightly built, darker-blond boy snorted in disgust, belying the look of unease in his blue eyes.

"Can't you pull off the road until this storm is over?" Joy implored her husband, laying a hand on his tense arm.

"I'm trying — I'm trying!" Skye said irritably. "But I can't just pull off on the shoulder. Visibility is almost nil and a car —

or truck — could hit us before they knew we were stopped."

Another brilliant blaze of lightning slashed the sky, followed by a ferocious crash of thunder. The girl in the back seat covered her ears and squeezed her eyes tightly closed.

But the boy leaned forward and spoke excitedly, "Do you see it, Dad? There's a wide place just ahead on the right."

"I see it! Hold on everyone; it may be bumpy."

The station wagon bounced over the rough ground, slipping and sliding through the mud as it plowed to a stop a short way off the highway.

"We may be stuck but at least we shouldn't get hit," Skye said with a sigh of relief. He laid his dark head back against the seat and stretched his long arms over his head.

"I'm still scared." Mitzie's voice quavered from the back seat after another bolt of lightning filled the dark afternoon sky. Thunder crashed and rumbled almost before the blaze disappeared from the sky.

"Don't be such a sissie!" Terry scoffed.

"That's enough, Terry. Don't badger your sister," his father said sternly, turning around to look at the children.

Terry, his thin face set in angry lines,

turned to stare into the sodden murk beyond the car window. He muttered, "She's not my sister!"

Flinching, as from a physical blow, Mitzie's wide blue eyes filled slowly with tears. She caught her lower lip between small white teeth to keep them from trembling as she laid her face against the coolness of the damp window glass. Skye and Joy looked helplessly at each other.

Silence reigned in the car as the storm's fury beat against them. They didn't see anyone else come by, and forty-five minutes later Joy's voice broke the sudden quiet.

"Look, the rain's stopped. The sun's coming out."

"These desert monsoon rains here in Arizona are really strange," Skye said. "It pours like Noah's flood and then suddenly stops. The sun comes out almost instantly — and the air's hotter than ever because of the humidity."

Joy rolled down her window and noticed that another vehicle — a battered Jeep with a canvas top — was parked a few yards behind them. As she watched, the door opened and a bronzed young man got out and stretched.

"We have a neighbor," Joy said softly to Skye.

The young man saw her eyes on him and grinned, showing strong white teeth and dark eyes that crinkled at the corners. Joy thought he had a rugged strength and attractiveness about him.

Joy smiled back, slightly embarrassed to be caught staring, then turned back to Skye. "Maybe we'll reach The Boulders before night after all. This part of Arizona is so desolate it gives me the shivers."

"We should," her husband said as he pushed open the car door, "but let's get out and stretch the kinks out before we go on."

Mitzie tumbled out of the car and looked around. Terry slid out the other side of the car and stood against it looking bored.

"Daddy, can I go over there and look at that big cactus?" Mitzie asked excitedly, pointing to a giant saguaro not far from them.

"Okay, but watch for snakes," Skye cautioned. He turned back toward Joy who had climbed out and was stretching luxuriously. He bent to place a gentle kiss on her lips, his dark eyes smiling into hers. "Come on, beautiful, and I'll find you a soft drink."

"I could certainly use one," Joy said emphatically as she slipped her hand into his.

"I want one, too," Terry said. He moved

14

toward the back of the station wagon. "I hate this steamy heat," he said sullenly.

Joy's sky-blue eyes were troubled as they rested upon Terry. When she and Skye had married three years before, both had thought the children would learn to love each other, but it hadn't happened.

Sipping the cold soft drink Skye had given her from the cooler, she remembered with a pang that, at first, her six-year-old Mitzie had been excited that she had a big brother. She had gone all out to win Terry's affection. But the nine-year-old Terry had made it plain that he didn't want a sister. His mother was dead — as was Mitzie's father — and he clearly did not want to share his father with anyone, except Joy. He had never resented her and had treated her with respect and love. Usually, he had ignored Mitzie, like a bad case of hives that he hoped would soon vanish.

But no longer! Joy had noticed a difference in Terry's attitude a few weeks before when the children had joined them in Mexico City. As soon as they arrived, Joy saw that Terry had changed. He never lost an opportunity to belittle Mitzie or to make fun of her.

Joy's eyes focused on her daughter. She was working her way toward the foot of a saguaro, skirting dripping palo verde trees and greasewood bushes. She saw Mitzie stop briefly to disengage her shirt from the thorns of a Cat's Claw bush before she moved on to gaze in awe at the towering desert giant.

Joy opened her mouth to call Mitzie when she heard her daughter scream in terror. Joy's heart lurched in fear as Mitzie turned and fled toward the car, stumbling and falling over bushes, screaming wildly.

Joy and Skye both dropped their soft drink cans and ran to meet the sobbing child. She had cleared the brush and was at the roadside before they reached her.

Mitzie fell into Joy's arms sobbing hysterically.

Skye knelt beside them and spoke gently but firmly, "What's wrong, Mitzie? What happened?"

When she continued to cry in great gasping sobs, Skye shook her arm, "Tell us, Mitzie. Are you all right? Did a snake or something bite you? Tell us!"

Mitzie began to shake her head violently, "No-o, no! N-nothing hurt me! I-I saw him. I looked down and saw him!"

"Saw who?" Skye asked.

Mitzie shuddered. "He-he's lying on the ground over there under that tall bush. My

16

heart nearly jumped out of my body when I saw him!"

"Who did you see?" a new voice said sharply. The dark, young man from the Jeep had appeared silently beside Skye. Terry stood just beyond him, the look of indifference replaced with alert interest.

"The-the body of a shriveled old man," Mitzie quavered. "His-his clothes are soaking wet, and his long grey hair is plastered to the wet ground."

She raised horrified eyes to her mother's face. "His-his eyes are w-wide open, and he was-was staring right at me. But-but his eyes don't even blink — or move at all — like they are-are dead!"

Without another word, the man turned and strode rapidly away toward the saguaro. Skye followed.

3

Skye and the young man knelt by a tall bush. The old man lay like a sodden bundle of rags. Skye lifted the thin, withered wrist, feeling for a pulse, knowing that he would find none.

When he heard a soft intake of breath, Skye turned quickly and saw Terry staring down into the open, vacant eyes of the dead man.

Joy and Mitzie were close enough to see the shape on the ground without seeing his face.

"W-what happened to th-the poor man?" Mitzie stammered.

The stranger squatted on his heels and leaned over the body to study the face.

"I would say this old man has been dead for quite some time."

"Do you know him?" Skye asked.

"No, but from the way he is dressed, I would say he's a wetback. You know, an illegal alien who's crossed over from Mexico."

"Mitzie, let's go back to the car," Joy urged.

"No, I want to know what happened to the poor man!" Mitzie's voice had a slightly hysterical tone.

The dark eyes the man turned on Mitzie were kind. "It's okay, little one," he said gently. "Don't worry about this old fellow. He doesn't even know he's wet and cold. Why don't you go to the car with your mother?"

He turned back to Skye. "I'm Paul Tanner. I live in the area. Would you stay here until I go down to a service station about a mile from here and call the police?"

"Sure thing," Skye readily agreed.

He and Paul began to walk back toward their cars with Terry trying to keep stride with his father. Joy and Mitzie moved more slowly behind them.

"I'm Skye Windthorn, and this is my wife, Joy, and our son and daughter, Terry and Mitzie."

Paul turned and acknowledged the introduction with a slight smile.

Mitzie hung back. "We're not just going to leave the poor d-dead man a-alone are we?" Her blue eyes were enormous.

"Honey, don't worry about the man," Skye said soothingly. "Paul was right. He is not feeling pain — or anything."

19

Mitzie, clinging to her mother's hand, turned back toward the car — then froze.

"W-what was that?"

Everyone stopped and stared at her.

"What was what?" Joy asked.

"I-I heard something — like a-a cry," Mitzie said through ashen lips.

"Aw, Mitzie, for goodness sakes!" Terry said, disgust obvious in his voice. "That's only the wind in the mesquite trees."

"It was not!" Mitzie's voice was angry. "I know what I heard!"

Joy looked at Paul's and Skye's faces, then down at her daughter.

Paul turned away and seemed to be searching the area with his eyes.

"Mitzie, you're just worked up," Skye said. "Go on to the car with your mother."

Mitzie took a step and then said excitedly, "There! There it was again! Did you hear it?"

"Hear what?" Terry said derisively.

Mitzie started to make a retort, but Paul intervened. "I heard something, too. It won't hurt to look. It could have been the moaning of the wind in the trees but — it could have been something else, too."

He began to walk slowly back toward where the old man's body was now hidden by the bushes and trees.

Skye hesitated for a moment as he watched Paul move away, then he said, "Terry — Mitzie, I want you to go with your mother to the car, and I want you to stay there. No arguments," he said firmly as he saw Terry frown and open his mouth to object.

Joy held her hand out to him, but Terry snapped his jaws shut and sullenly headed for the car ahead of Joy and Mitzie.

The heat was steamy and oppressive and the hot wind stirred up bits of sand that stung their faces and made their eyes smart as they crossed the road to the station wagon.

"They're completely nuts for looking for anything," Terry said as he slouched down in the backseat. "There's nothing out there. It's just dopey Mitzie's big imagination."

"It won't hurt to check," Joy said.

"We're wasting our time when we could be on the road with the air-conditioner on!" Terry replied in disgust.

"There's Daddy," Mitzie cried suddenly. "And he's running. Something must be wrong!"

All three piled out of the car as Skye sprinted across the road and came up to the car breathing hard.

"What's wrong?"

Joy followed Skye as he dashed to the back of the car and opened the back door.

"There's a girl out there!" Skye said between gasps for breath. "She's not dead, but she looks bad." He jerked out a gallon thermos jug of water and a blanket and dashed away.

Joy, Terry, and Mitzie followed Skye back into the desert brush.

The girl lay under the scanty shade of a palo verde tree in a small recess in the ground a couple of hundred yards from the highway.

As they neared the spot, they heard her soft moaning, carried on the hot desert wind. It was a sound that lifted the hair on the back of Joy's neck and prickled down her spine. It was a sound charged with hopelessness and despair.

4

Paul raised the girl's head and Skye held the thermos cup to her lips. Long, water-soaked dark hair clung to her face and straggled across the sand. A coarse cotton blouse and skirt, sodden with water and mud, covered her frail body. The girl swallowed a little water, then choked. Paul raised her head higher as she sputtered and coughed, lifting her hands weakly to cover her mouth.

Recovering from her fit of coughing, the girl's eyes opened — wide, dark, frightened. She struggled to sit up but didn't seem to have the strength. The dark-lashed eyelids came swiftly down to cover her eyes and she fell back against Paul's arm.

"Do you have anything nourishing in your car? Fruit juice or milk?" Skye asked Paul. "We usually do, but today we only have soft drinks."

"Fruit juice," Paul said, "I'll go get it."

"I'll help you," Terry offered.

"Me, too," Mitzie said eagerly.

23

"We don't need you, Mitzie," Terry said, glowering.

"I'm going, too," Mitzie insisted.

"Both of you can help," Paul said, ignoring Terry's scowl. Gently he lowered the girl's head to the rapidly drying ground. "Let's go." The three set off at a trot toward the cars.

"*Por favor* . . ." The girl's weak voice caught Joy's attention. Her frightened eyes were upon Joy.

Joy leaned over her and spoke softly in Spanish, "Do you speak English?"

The girl moved her head from side to side, "No-no English," she said weakly in Spanish.

"Talk to her, Skye," Joy implored. "You speak Spanish so much better than I do."

Skye nodded and spoke softly, "Don't be afraid, we want to help you. We'll have some juice for you right away. Just lie still and rest."

But fear stared out of her eyes as they flitted from Skye to Joy. Her voice was a thin thread of distress, "Conchita . . ."

"*Si*, Conchita . . . ?" Skye asked gently.

"I am Luana. They have my sister, Conchita," the girl whispered.

"Who has your sister?"

"The *coyotes!*"

"Didn't she say the *coyotes* have her sister?" Joy asked Skye incredulously.

24

"Yes — but I don't think she means the four-legged kind," Skye said grimly. He spoke a few quick words to Luana, and she slowly nodded her head.

"She means the smugglers that illegal aliens pay to bring them across the border into the United States. She said two *coyotes* took her sister away and left all the others to die."

"You mean they took your money and brought a bunch of you out here in the desert and left you to die?" Joy spoke directly to Luana in her halting Spanish.

"*Si,* there were ten of us. They are all scattered back there," Luana's dark eyes mirrored horror and pain. Her anguished whisper was barely audible. "Dead, I think."

"Why did they take Conchita?" Skye probed gently.

For a moment Luana closed her eyes and took a deep breath as if she didn't have the strength to speak.

"You don't have to talk," Joy said softly.

But after a moment, she opened her eyes which had flooded with tears, "Conchita is only fifteen . . . and very pretty. She talked much with the *coyote* called Pascual, and he took her with them."

"Surely she did not know they were leaving you to die," Joy said.

"She tried to get the *coyotes* to take me,

too, but they refused. They did give me a small canteen of water, though — to please Conchita, I think. I shared it with the others so it did not last long," Luana whispered.

"Would you like some more water?" Skye asked, pouring out another cupful when she nodded.

Joy lifted the cup of water to Luana's lips. She drank slowly until it was all gone, then closed her eyes.

"Will we have to turn her in to the police?" Joy asked Skye in English.

"I'm afraid so," Skye said.

"But they'll send her back to Mexico!"

"I know," Skye said, "but it can't be helped."

Luana suddenly opened her eyes and spoke fearfully in Spanish.

"What did she say?" Joy asked.

"She said, 'You aren't *coyotes,* are you?' "

"No, of course we aren't smugglers!" Joy said to Luana.

"Then why are you with that other one?"

"You mean Paul? We just met him," Skye said. "He was parked in his Jeep at the rest area."

"*Si, si,* in his Jeep! That one — the other *coyotes* called him *La Vibora* — he was in a Jeep down there, too! He is a *coyote*," Luana declared as emphatically as she could.

Glancing back toward the parking area where Paul, Terry, and Mitzie had disappeared, then back at the girl, Joy exclaimed, "Surely not! He seems like a very nice man and very helpful."

"Where did you mean when you said you saw him 'down there'?" Skye asked.

"In Sonoita, on the Mexican side of the border, where we met with the *coyotes*," Luana said.

Joy suddenly stiffened. "The children! They went with him to the car. He wouldn't harm them, would he?"

Skye jumped to his feet and started toward the car, but he hadn't gone far when Paul, Terry, and Mitzie came around the high, screening brush and trees, walking swiftly.

When he saw Skye coming toward them, Paul also broke into a run. "Is the girl worse?" he called.

"No, no, but . . . we do need to get some nourishment into her." As soon as Paul knelt beside her, Luana's dark eyes darted to his face, then turned to hold Joy's eyes.

Joy gripped the frightened girl's hand and said gently, "Don't be afraid, we are your friends. We won't let anything happen to you. Now, drink some juice."

Luana took the cup of juice Joy poured for her in trembling hands. With Joy steadying

27

her hands, she drained it greedily. *"Muchas gracias,"* she said softly.

She handed the cup to Joy with a slightly steadier hand and whispered anxiously, "Will you help me find my sister?"

Paul squatted on the soles of his booted feet. "What is she saying?"

"You don't speak Spanish?" Skye asked. "I would have thought you were at least part Spanish."

Paul laughed lightly. "Lots of people do. I have just enough Indian blood to darken my skin. I wish I could speak Spanish — I live so close to Mexico. I just never bothered to learn. Oh, I understand a word here and there but not much."

He looked down at Luana and repeated his question, "What did she ask you?"

When Luana saw his eyes on her, she instantly let her dark lashes sweep down to cover her eyes, and she was silent.

"She asked if we could help her find her sister. She says the smugglers brought her and nine others over from Mexico. They took her sister and left the others to die," Skye said, closely watching Paul's face. "She also said you were one of the *coyotes* . . . that she saw you with them in Sonoita, Mexico, and that you are called the viper, by the *coyotes.*"

Paul looked astonished, then threw back his dark head and laughed. "I'm a *coyote?* That girl's loco. I've never been to Sonoita. I stick to the good old United States, myself. She's got me mixed up with someone else."

Then he sobered. "Why don't you ask the girl what the names of the smugglers are."

Skye nodded, then spoke softly to Luana, "What are the smugglers' names? If you can remember, it might help us find the ones who took your sister."

The girl opened her eyes and looked fearfully at Paul and then at Skye. Her voice was barely audible and shook slightly as she said, "Tiberio and Pascual."

"I don't know anyone by those names around here," Paul said. "But I suppose they would be Mexicans from across the border, anyway."

He stared at Luana curiously for a moment, then stood up. "Did she say anything that might indicate where they took her sister?"

Skye repeated the question in Spanish to Luana, but she shook her head. Joy and Skye rose to their feet.

"Where are you folks headed?" Paul asked.

Skye answered, "A friend of mine has a large home near here. We are to be his houseguests for a few weeks while I do some work."

"What kind of work do you do?"

"I'm an archaeologist, and I work on ancient manuscripts."

Paul grinned. "Then you must be the guests of Richard Borders at The Boulders. Everyone knows he is interested in archaeology and owns some priceless artifacts."

"His home sounds fascinating," Joy said. "I'm looking forward to seeing it."

"It is," Paul said. "He's my neighbor — though my little house is humble indeed compared to his." His grin faded, "Perhaps I should take the young woman to my house since it isn't far. I have a phone, and I could call the police from there. There could be someone else out there alive who needs help."

"How far is it to The Boulders?" Skye asked.

"Maybe ten miles," Paul replied.

"Why don't we just take the girl there," Skye said. "I'm sure Richard won't mind."

Paul shrugged his shoulders. "As you wish. I'll stay here with the body of the old man. Be sure to notify the police. I have a folding cot in my Jeep that would make an excellent stretcher for the girl. I'll go get it." He loped away toward his vehicle.

Suddenly Luana's weak voice whispered from the ground, "You aren't going to let him take me anywhere, are you? I am so afraid of that man!"

"Don't you worry," Joy said, stooping to pat her hand. "We won't let him take you anywhere!"

5

Hot air surged into the car when Skye rolled down the station wagon window at The Boulders guardhouse — set into a high rock wall — and handed the uniformed guard his card.

"I'll call the house." The attendant withdrew into an obviously air-conditioned room, lifted the phone to his ear, and conferred briefly. Stepping out, he said respectfully, "You're expected, Dr. Windthorn."

The huge metal gate divided silently and slid outward.

Skye guided the car through the gate and along a paved road that sloped upward into the rocks.

"This *is* impressive," Joy breathed ecstatically.

Most of the estate inside the encircling high wall appeared to be a wide, high hill of huge, tumbled boulders. Royal palms lined the curving driveway and ahead of them they glimpsed the feathery fronds of date palms bending under the desert wind's constant assault.

The car curved around mammoth boulders and came out into a circular driveway. The dark green of juniper shrubbery and piñon trees mingled with the prickly beauty of several varieties of cactus bordering the circle of the drive.

"The house is built right into the hill among the boulders," Mitzie said excitedly. "Don't you just love it?"

A small, silver-haired man came swiftly down the wide circular steps from the portico as the station wagon stopped. He was immaculately dressed in a cream-colored suit, soft brown shirt and cream tie. His smile, under a trim mustache, was warm and welcoming.

"Skye! This is such a pleasure!" he exclaimed. "Come on in out of the heat before I meet your family."

Skye jumped out of the car and met him at the bottom step and wrung his hand. "It's good to see you again, Richard," Skye said warmly, then he lowered his voice. "We have a small problem."

Skye quickly related what had happened. "She needs medical attention immediately."

"She's an illegal alien," Richard said thoughtfully. "Did she say where she is from — and who brought her into the States?"

"I'm presuming she's from Mexico since

she came across the border from there," Skye said. "She's very weak so she hasn't talked much. She spoke of crossing the border at Sonoita and that two of the smugglers who brought her party over were called Pascual and Tiberio."

"All the others of her party are dead?"

"She thinks so. However, we should alert the police immediately. There is a remote chance someone else is alive. I hope it won't be an imposition to let the girl rest here until we can get an ambulance to take her to a hospital," Skye finished.

"No problem at all," his host said. "And we're in luck. A physician friend of mine, Cyrus Bennett, is visiting me for a few days. We'll ask him to look at her."

Turning toward the house entrance, he snapped his fingers at a young, smartly uniformed male servant standing near the doorway.

"Rafael, get Tomas. There's a girl in the station wagon who needs to be carried inside."

"We have a folding cot for a stretcher," Skye said.

While the two servants and Skye were gently loading Luana onto the makeshift stretcher, Richard greeted Joy, Mitzie, and Terry, inviting them inside out of the heat.

Wide, carved double doors led into a spacious room. Richard directed Rafael, Tomas, and Skye to place Luana on a plump chaise lounge. Urging everyone to be seated, he ordered a maid to bring them refreshments, then hurried away to call the police and an ambulance.

Joy noticed that Luana lay still and silent, her long heavy lashes stark against her pale face. Moving quickly to her side, Joy drew up a cushioned chair and spoke slowly so she could form her thoughts into Spanish, "How are you feeling, Luana?"

The girl's eyes came open as if with great effort. She seemed to have trouble focusing on Joy. "I-I am so very tired."

"A doctor will be here soon to help you."

"P-please don't let them . . . make me go back . . . home until I find Conchita," Luana pled weakly. "I must find . . . Conchita." The words trailed off, but Luana's eyes held Joy's captive.

"I'll do my best," Joy promised. "Could you drink something?"

"*Si, gracias,*" she whispered.

"I'll get her something, Mother," Mitzie offered and ran over to a little table that held a pitcher of iced tea and a plate of cookies.

Distracted, Joy saw Terry standing near the table with a cookie in one hand and a glass of tea in the other. "Mama's little helper," Terry said scornfully in a voice Joy knew he had not meant for her to hear. She saw Mitzie duck her head and turn away so quickly that the tray dipped dangerously and tea sloshed out onto the napkin and cookie. Both were wet as Mitzie handed them to her, trying to avoid her eyes.

But Joy saw the tears that had welled up in her daughter's eyes.

Unable to leave Luana to correct Terry, Joy smoothed Mitzie's hair back from her face and tried to comfort her with a gentle smile. Their eyes met, and then broke off as Luana moaned slightly.

"Oh, Luana, I'm sorry," Joy exclaimed. "Here. This is iced tea."

Luana curved long, slim fingers around the tea glass and tried to bring it to her lips, but her hands trembled so badly that Mitzie steadied them while Joy held her head up from the pillow so she could drink.

"Thank you." The words were weak, soft. Lying back, Luana's dark eyes roamed the room, growing wide, *"Señora,* never have I seen a house like this one! It is *magnifico!"*

"It is beautiful," Joy agreed. For the first time she really looked at the room.

In the center of a floor paved in natural flagstones, a fountain sent showers of spar-

36

kling droplets cascading into a pool where bright fish darted among water lilies and greenery. A gleaming brass chandelier hung high overhead like an artificial sun. Large pots of flowering plants, shrubs, and small trees made a delightful background for the sofas, chairs, and small tables that were colorful splashes of color about the room.

More intriguing yet were two boulders which rose from the floor to blend into the decor of the huge room. It was from around them that Joy saw their host come striding back into the room with a pink-faced, cherub-like man in tow. Richard motioned toward the girl lying on the lounge, and the new arrival moved briskly to her side and set down the dark brown bag he carried.

Skye and Terry moved across the room, and Richard introduced Dr. Bennett to the Windthorns.

The doctor acknowledged the introductions with a quick nod of his partially bald, pink head. Opening his case, he brought out a stethoscope and hung it around his pudgy neck.

"Let's give the doctor some space." Richard led the Windthorns to the table where the refreshments were laid out. Waving them all to comfortable chairs, he sank into a cushioned armchair, took a quick sip from his tea glass, set it down, and turned to Skye.

"I have a friend, Bob Lawson, who is connected with Immigration. A very influential man. I have spoken with him."

Richard smiled. "I was touched when you told me the smugglers had taken this young woman's sister. She must be found — quickly — or there is no telling what will happen to her. Perhaps Luana — I believe you said her name is — can give us more information to help in the search. Bob wants her kept right here until she is well enough to talk with Immigration officials.

"I turned the whole case over to him. He will begin a thorough search immediately for the other Mexican illegals and will do everything possible to find that poor girl's sister."

"It's very kind of you to allow Luana to stay here," Joy said. "She was terrified of being sent back home before she found her sister."

Richard grimaced. "I'm afraid she will have to be sent back — but Bob can delay it temporarily."

The doctor crossed the floor to them and spoke to the group. "With good care, the girl should recover completely. But she must have a great deal of rest, lots of liquids, and, later, some good solid food.

"If she could be moved to a quiet room now, I will see what I can do to make her more comfortable. The sun, heat, and thirst have played havoc in her body. Her legs and feet, and even her arms and hands are loaded with cactus spines which I should remove."

"Poor little thing. May I stay with her until she falls asleep?" Joy asked. "She's terribly frightened."

"Certainly," Dr. Bennett said as he went back to his patient.

Richard gave a quick order in Spanish to a hovering houseboy, and the young man hurried away. He turned back to Skye. "Ruiz will take care of moving the girl to a quiet room so why don't we get you settled in your rooms."

He turned a quick smile upon Mitzie and Terry. "When you are settled in, I want you to meet my daughter, Veronica. She's fourteen, a little older than you, Terry, but I hope you will be friends."

"I'd like to meet her," Terry said politely.

"I didn't know you had a daughter," Skye said.

Richard's face sobered. "Veronica's been at boarding schools in the winters and at camps during the summer for most of her life. Her mother — isn't well, and spends much of her time in hospitals and convalescent homes.

"I've been too busy to have Veronica home much. But recently my wife has been in Tucson in a. . . ." His voice turned suddenly bitter. "I don't suppose there's any use hiding it. She's in a de-tox hospital. For years she has been fighting a losing battle with alcohol."

"I'm sorry," Skye said. "I had no idea."

"I should be used to it by this time," Richard said heavily. "Anyway, since Monica is in a hospital near here, she wanted me to keep Veronica home for awhile — get acquainted with her."

He laughed without mirth. "I've hardly ever been around the child. I've been so busy making money — to keep Monica in her hospitals and convalescent homes getting dried out — I haven't had time. And now I'm suddenly expected to act like a father!"

Joy knew her expressive face showed shock, which she quickly tried to mask. Skye looked distinctly uncomfortable.

Richard's face twisted in the semblance of a grin. "I suppose this tirade surprises you two. But you see, I never wanted a child — and I don't think Monica did either. Having an alcoholic wife has been enough strain. I suppose you will think me callous, but I left Veronica's care to others when her mother was away, which was often. I don't even know the girl."

"You've missed out on a lot," Joy said gently.

Richard studied Joy's face briefly. "I'm not sure every man is cut out to be a father. Even when my daughter was small I never knew what to say to her. She didn't seem to like me then, and I don't think she does now. But she's stuck with me until I can arrange to send her to a summer camp."

He took a deep breath. "But enough about us. Let's get you settled."

6

A few minutes later Terry was placing folded shirts in a dresser drawer when a husky female voice spoke from the partly open door.

"May I come in?"

"Sure," Terry said, turning curiously.

Pale brown hair like spun honey framed emerald green eyes, sparkling and heavily mascaraed. She surveyed him from beneath dark, arched brows.

"Hi!" The petite figure encased in fitted, bright orange coveralls sank gracefully into a chair near the door. "I'm Veronica, but call me Nica for short. I hate Veronica."

"But-but," Terry stammered. "I thought you were just a-a kid. You're a-a. . . ." His face flooded with color, and he stopped abruptly. This girl looked at least seventeen!

". . . A woman?" The full red lips parted in a pleased smile, showing perfect white teeth. "I wish my mother — and dear old Papa — could see that. To them I'm just a child, to order around and send off to some dull girl's school whenever it pleases them."

She laughed softly. "Not that their old schools want me for long. I was kicked out of three — of the most expensive and exclusive — this past year."

Her amused chuckle came again. "When I got thrown out of the last one three weeks before school was out, my own dear mama made me come home. So now Papa's wondering what to do with me!"

During this discourse, Terry stood uncertainly by the dresser with a pair of socks in one hand, shifting uncomfortably.

"You don't need to put away your own clothes," Nica said. "That's what we have servants for."

"Oh, I don't mind," Terry began, "I . . ."

"Come on with me and I'll show you around," Nica insisted. "I'll ring for one of the maids to unpack for you."

She pressed a buzzer on the wall and moved toward the door. "You're not nearly as old as I am, but I'm so bored I'd welcome an infant if it could talk."

"I'm *almost* as old as you are!" Terry said stiffly, sudden anger lancing through him. "Your father said you're fourteen and I'm almost thirteen!"

Nica laughed, her husky voice silky. "Sorry, I didn't mean to insult you. I forget that girls usually grow faster than boys. For-

43

give me?" She smiled, a deep dimple appearing as if by magic in one slim, smooth cheek.

"It's okay," Terry mumbled.

"Okay, then, let's go."

Terry followed her reluctantly. Something about this girl both repelled and drew him. He knew some girls at school but he didn't feel comfortable around any of them — and they were just ordinary girls. He hadn't been around this one more than two minutes, but he already knew there was nothing ordinary about her!

He sensed a wildness about Richard Borders' daughter. Barely suppressed excitement seemed to flow from her dancing eyes: challenging, daring, and a little scary.

As his feet lagged at the door of his room, a blonde maid came hurrying up. "Margie," Veronica instructed her quickly, "unpack and put away Terry's belongings."

"Now," Nica said as the maid went into Terry's room, "let's go explore."

Terry was quickly lost as Veronica guided him through the strangest, yet most elegant, house he had ever seen. Windthorn, his home in the wilderness of Idaho was considered a mansion, but this place had real atmosphere. The rooms and halls were built into the hill, some woven right in among

44

massive boulders. Several rooms had walls formed by the side of a boulder.

Hallways connected the chambers, and there were many stone stairways that climbed or descended without any apparent design. Some led to rooms — many with skylights and others with almost solid walls of draperied glass doors — while others opened to the outdoors.

One sliding glass door opened to reveal an isolated hideaway that contained two cushioned lounge chairs on the edge of a tiny green pool. A miniature waterfall tumbled down over rough stones into the pool.

At last, when Terry was thoroughly lost, they climbed a stairway and stepped out onto a large sundeck, built of redwood across a large boulder, furnished with a stone barbeque grill, assorted hardwood chairs, and a picnic table. Stone steps, carpeted with stone-colored outdoor carpet, led down to a lavish pool area.

He and Veronica descended the stairs and went through sliding doors onto a tiled floor. The silvery-green water of the pool rippled over rugged rocks before splashing into the swimming pool. A large flat boulder where swimmers could rest rose from near the center. A high, green dome covered the whole pool area.

"The water would get too hot to be comfortable if it wasn't covered," Nica explained.

"It's awfully pretty," Terry said. "Do you swim here a lot?"

Veronica stared moodily at the water for a moment and a visible shudder ran through her slim body. "Not at all! I don't like it! I-I don't know why, but there is something about this pool that-that scares me silly. And it's not that I'm afraid of water. I swim like a duck. It's just something about this pool."

Abruptly, she turned her back on the pool. Grabbing Terry's hand, she started tugging him toward a double door to their left. "Come with me, I want to show you something that will really blow your mind!"

Terry felt a chill run down his spine. There was a small, taunting smile on Nica's face, and her eyes shone with a reckless, daredevil glitter.

For a moment Terry resisted the pull of her hand, and Nica stopped suddenly. Her lips twisted. "You're afraid! I thought you were adventuresome and daring, but I guess I was wrong. You're nothing but a baby!"

Her goading mockery cut through Terry like a serrated knife. Sensitive about his small stature and unable to stand ridicule of any kind, he pushed away the chill that filled him. He straightened to his full height and said as cuttingly as he could, "You'd cry before I would!"

A smug little smile flashed over Nica's face. She cast a quick look about and lowered her voice. "You must first promise me that you won't tell a soul what you are about to see. We could both be in extreme danger if we get caught. Will you promise to tell no one? Absolutely no one!"

Her eyes seemed to change subtly. Was there fear mingled with the reckless, devil-may-care light that danced in her emerald eyes?

Terry felt his heart banging in fright beneath his shirt, but Nica's exhilarating, daring, and reckless abandonment seemed contagious. Suddenly, he felt his veins pulsing with excitement.

"I promise!"

Veronica's hand grabbed his again. It was cold now. Was it trembling?

She led him rapidly through a series of short halls, always descending, until they were in what appeared to be a storage area. They moved silently past several closed doors and stopped at a corner.

Before Nica entered the new hallway, she peered cautiously around the corner and then moved on. Terry stayed close behind her, walking as softly as she. It was eerily quiet and even their whispery footsteps on the stone paving seemed loud in the total silence. Lamps set in the rock walls only dimly lighted the hall.

Suddenly Nica stopped before a door and put a finger to her lips. Her eyes looked dark green in her pale face as she listened intently at the door for a full moment. Then glancing back the way they had come, she drew a key from her pocket and opened the heavy door.

Stepping in, she quickly pulled Terry into the blackness and closed the door. Listening to her labored breathing, Terry felt his throat constrict until he felt he couldn't swallow or breathe. He sensed her fear like a tangible, living thing.

Nica moved slightly and a dim light — like a night light — flashed on. She groped her way across the room, flipped another switch, and the room was flooded with white, searing light.

Terry shaded his eyes from the overpowering light with his hand until they adjusted and then he stared in disbelief. "Wh-what is this place?" he stuttered.

The walls were draped in black curtains. At the front of the room, large five-pointed stars splashed blood-red against the black drapery. A red-draped lectern stood beneath the pentagram symbols.

Terry unconsciously drew back toward the door as his eyes rested on a black draped coffin-like box. Arranged on its length were black candles and large, blood-red goblets. A dozen or so chairs, shrouded in black, were arranged in a semi-circle on the scarlet-carpeted floor.

A strange light flamed in Nica's eyes as she said softly and triumphantly, "Didn't I tell you it would blow your mind? It's the worship room for a satanic cult!"

She leaned over and flicked off the bright light, plunging the room back into eerie gloom. Her voice sounded hollow and unreal in the unearthly silence. "We'd better get out of here."

Her cold hand clutched his and pulled him out the door. As she quickly locked it, she whispered, "Did you see those stains on the altar? I'm sure they were blood."

7

Terry started down the dim passageway ahead of Veronica, goosebumps racing over his skin. The sooner he got out of this creepy place the better! But before he had taken three steps, Nica hauled him to an abrupt stop.

Her head close to his, she whispered words that sent shivers down his spine. "I think I saw something move down at the corner ahead. Do — do you have any kind of weapon?"

Terry fumbled with frightened fingers in his pocket and came up with a small pen knife. "That's all I have. But-but surely you don't think anyone would actually hurt us in your own house?" he whispered.

"I don't know. We're a long way from the main part of the house and — and safety. I've only been back at The Boulders a month, but I know some strange things are going on around here," she whispered back. She clutched his arm with cold, tense fingers.

"Let me have the knife," Nica said softly. Before Terry could protest, Nica took it from his nerveless fingers.

"Now let's go quietly to the end of the hall. If anyone attacks us, we'll give him the battle of his life!" Nica's face was pale in the dim light but the danger-intoxication Terry had sensed earlier in Nica rang once more in her voice.

With pounding heart, Terry catfooted down the hall beside Nica, surreptitiously wiping his perspiration-slick palms on his jeans legs.

At the end of the hallway, he peered around the corner. Drawing back, he spoke softly, "There's no one there. Maybe you just imagined you saw someone. The light is awfully dim."

Nica moved around the corner and stood staring through the gloom of the passageway. "I didn't imagine it," she said crossly. "I have very good eyes. Besides, I'm almost certain I heard footsteps — real faint — like someone didn't want to be heard."

"It doesn't matter," Terry said quickly. "Let's get out of this place. It gives me the creeps!"

Nica stared at him in the semi-darkness for a moment, then said softly, "Remember, you promised to not tell a soul about this place. Not your parents, or your sister or anyone."

"I don't go back on a promise," Terry said stiffly. "And don't call Mitzie my sister! I don't have a sister!"

Quick interest flared in Nica's eyes. "Father said you had a sister. If Mitzie isn't your sister, who is she?"

"Just my stepmother's daughter, that's all!"

"She's your stepsister then, whether you'll admit it or not," Nica said impishly.

"I don't claim her, so she's not!"

Nica studied Terry for a moment with an amused expression in her emerald eyes. Then, abruptly, she changed the subject, "We had better get out of here." She started down the passageway at a jog, treading lightly on the balls of her feet.

Joy was coming out of the door to her room when she saw Terry and a strange girl coming down the hall toward his room. Polite and every ounce the little hostess as she acknowledged Terry's introduction, Nica expressed how pleased she was to have them at The Boulders. Then she excused herself and went away, walking sedately and gracefully like a young lady.

"What a charming girl," Joy said, watching

her go. "And she looks much older than four-teen. She will be good company for you, Terry."

"I suppose," Terry said doubtfully.

Joy studied him in a puzzled way for a moment and then said, "Dinner will be served in thirty minutes. The meal will be casual so you'll only need to dress in a nice shirt and slacks."

"Okay," Terry said and turned away.

"Wait, Terry," Joy said. When he turned back with a questioning look, she continued, a worried expression on her gentle face. "I know you are older than Mitzie, and brothers often don't want to be bothered with little sisters, but I can't help notice that things are not going well at all between you and Mitzie. You seem to go out of your way anymore to needle her. I want to help, Terry. Has something happened between you two that you need to talk about?"

Joy saw a closed look drop down over Terry's face, and he no longer met her gaze directly.

"I hadn't noticed I was needling her. I'll try to do better." He turned abruptly. "I'd better get dressed. Don't want to be late." He walked swiftly down the hall to his room.

With a sigh, Joy went back into her room. *Father, what can I do? He shuts me out if I even suggest there is anything wrong between him and Mitzie,* she prayed. *If only he would talk to me!*

She had discussed — or attempted to — the matter of the children's relationship with Skye, but he had never felt there was a real problem. At first he had said to give them time, and later he said big brothers didn't often show much attention to little sisters. Even lately, when he caught Terry saying hateful things to Mitzie, he reprimanded him but passed it off to Joy as, "the boy is going into that difficult teenage period."

Maybe I am overly anxious about them. Perhaps Veronica will be good for him, she mused as she dressed for dinner. *She seems like such a sweet, mature young lady. And she seems to be taking an interest in Terry. Maybe she will be just what he needs — a positive big sister image.*

8

Luana was sitting up in bed the next morning, a glow on her thin face. "*Señor* Borders says he is already trying to find my sister. Also, the *señor* says I can work for him right here in his beautiful *hacienda* until Conchita is found."

"Wonderful! That is so kind of him," Joy said in Spanish, slowly, so she could pull the right words from her memory. "But you aren't going to work right away, are you? You're still so weak; you nearly died in the desert!"

"I am much stronger already," Luana assured her. "The doctor gave me something to make me sleep, and I feel so much better this morning. In a day or so I think I can work." Tears suddenly rose in her dark, expressive eyes. "The *señor* is so very kind. I want to pay for my food and shelter as soon as I am able."

"Is this to be your room?" Joy asked, as she cast her eyes about the small, clean, but sparsely-furnished room.

"*Si!*" Luana cried happily. "Is it not fine? I never had a room all my own before." Her voice grew wistful. "If only I could stay in America! Conchita and I dreamed about this for years while we worked hard and saved to pay a *coyote* to bring us across the border."

A lump formed in Joy's throat and she said quickly, "Did *Señor* Borders say what he is doing to get your sister back?"

Trust shone in Luana's eyes. "No, but he told me not to worry, that he would get her back."

Joy was tempted to tell Luana not to get her hopes too high, but swallowed the words before they were uttered. Luana had gone through so much. She didn't need discouragement right now.

Heavenly Father, please bring Conchita back to this poor girl, she prayed silently. *Richard's power is limited but yours is not. Please watch over her and bring her back safely.*

Suddenly Luana reached out and grasped Joy's hand tightly in her own. "There is only one thing that worries me."

"What is that?" Joy asked gently.

"Paul Tanner! He-he could not harm me here, could he?"

"Of course not!" Joy said emphatically. "You're as safe here as it is humanly possible to be. There are guards at the gates and security of all kinds. Besides, perhaps you were mistaken about Paul. He said you have him mixed up with someone else."

"I do not think so," Luana said slowly. "This morning I was lying here in bed, and suddenly I remembered something. As I was dying of heat and thirst out on the desert, I heard the motor of a car, running slowing as if it were searching for someone. I believed the *coyotes* were returning so I hid and that's the last I remember."

She drew a shuddering breath. "Then a short time later who should show up where I was but Paul Tanner! I remember him well as the one the *coyotes* called the viper, because, . . ." suddenly she dropped her eyes, "because I thought he was good-looking.

"Don't you see, *Señora* Windthorn," she said, looking up again, "he must be one of the smuggler ring — out looking for any of us who didn't die! To see that no one lived to tell what a horrible crime they did!"

Joy squeezed Luana's hand. "You will probably never see him again anyway so don't you worr. . . ." She broke off as she heard Luana gasp. Luana's hand gripped Joy's convulsively as she stared through fear-filled eyes at the door.

Joy swung around. Just beyond Skye in the doorway stood Paul Tanner.

As the two men moved into the room, Joy saw that Paul had exchanged his soiled clothing for clean jeans and a blue western shirt. He looked neat and shaven. Even his brown western boots were polished.

Brushing a lock of straight black hair off his forehead with a flick of one tanned hand, his dark, alert eyes swept the small room before they settled upon Luana's tense figure in the bed.

The lean face lost its hardness as his thin lips parted in a smile, showing strong, white teeth.

"Do you remember Paul?" Skye asked Luana. At her quick, frightened nod, he continued, "He came to see how you are."

Her long lashes dropped and she said softly in Spanish, "Tell him I am fine and thank him for coming."

After Skye relayed the message, Joy watched Paul study the girl for a moment, then shift his dark, inscrutable eyes to Skye, who had moved to stand beside Joy.

"I thought you all might be interested to know about the others. I stayed and helped the Border Patrol and sheriff's department in the search. We found eight illegals in all, including the old man that we found."

"Were they all dead?" Joy asked.

Paul nodded his head. "I'm afraid so. The

poor fools never had a chance." His eyes and voice betrayed deep anger.

"You can't blame them for trying to better themselves," Joy said.

"I suppose not," Paul said, "but to put their lives in the hands of greedy, ruthless men they never met before is just asking for it!" His dark eyes seemed to smolder.

Suddenly he smiled and the anger vanished. *His rugged face is almost handsome when he smiles,* Joy thought. But she sensed a deep-seated turbulence about the man that troubled her . . . even frightened her.

As Skye relayed to Luana the news of the search — and that all of the illegals were found dead, Joy studied Paul covertly.

Could this lean, bronzed man be a *coyote?* He spoke with contempt of those who used the smugglers. But his anger didn't seem directed at the *coyotes.* Could he be sympathetic with them because he was one? Perhaps he considered himself a good one. But smuggling illegals into the United States was a crime, even if it was done humanely.

"What do you do for a living, Paul?" Joy asked suddenly when Skye had finished the brief narration of the search to Luana.

Paul's dark eyes swung to Joy's face and seemed to study her before he answered carelessly, "Oh, I raise a few cattle on my little ranch and do odd jobs for some of the ranchers around. I get by."

"You aren't married?" Joy couldn't resist asking.

Paul looked startled for a moment and then laughed outright. "I'm not that dumb!" He hesitated, then hastened to add, "Not that it isn't okay for some people. But marriage just wouldn't work for me."

Abruptly he turned to Skye, "The police and Border Patrol did not mention the girl here, so I presume you didn't tell them about Luana when you called them about the dead Mexican?" His statement was a question.

"I didn't notify the police or Border Patrol," Skye said. "Our host, Richard Borders did. Or I should say he called a friend — Bob Lawson, who is connected with Immigration — and had him take care of it."

"I didn't mention the girl either when no one asked me about her," Paul said. "I thought you might have a reason for keeping her presence here a secret."

Skye laughed. "Nothing deep and dark, I assure you. Mr. Borders turned the whole case over to his friend, Bob Lawson, who requested that the girl be kept here for questioning."

Paul shrugged. "I was just curious."

"Richard told Luana she can work for him as soon as she is able," Joy supplied. "He's also promised to help her find her sister, Conchita."

"Nice man," Paul said.

"Perhaps there's one thing that neither Mr. Borders nor any of us have considered," Paul continued. "Luana is the only one who can identify the *coyotes*. She could be in danger. These men are not just smugglers of people. They also kidnapped a young girl and are holding her captive somewhere — if she hasn't been abused and murdered and then dumped out in the desert where she may never be found!"

"Surely they wouldn't kill her!" Joy exclaimed.

"Why not?" Paul's dark eyes were as bleak and hard as black flint. "They killed five men and three women as surely as if they had put a gun to their heads — and certainly not as humanely. It isn't their fault that Luana escaped the same fate."

"You're right," Skye said. "I'll ask Richard to do all he can to protect her. But she should be safe here. This place is like a fortress."

Skye was thoughtful for a moment, then added, "But don't you think the smugglers probably headed back to Mexico as soon as they dumped their victims in the desert?"

"Possibly," Paul said. "But if they are part of a ring or into other crimes as well, it's anybody's guess where they are. Maybe even right here, working as servants. How do we know? Smuggling is a nice, lucrative sideline. It wouldn't hurt to keep an eye on her yourselves while you are here."

He rose to go. "I'd better be getting back to work. I'm taking a few cattle in to the sale today." He politely — through Skye — wished Luana a rapid recovery of both her health and her sister. Lifting a hand to Joy, he started out the door.

"You can take your folding cot back with you," Skye said, following him out into the hall. "It's in my station wagon. I'll get it for you."

"There's no need for that," a voice said. Richard Borders stood by the door. "I'll have one of the servants get it for the young man on the way out."

Richard stepped toward Paul. "So you are my neighbor, Paul Tanner." He extended his hand and smiled. "Skye told me that you live a few miles from me — and that you were in on their little adventure."

"Yes, sir," Paul said, gripping the older man's hand and returning his smile. "I hope you don't mind my coming to see how the girl is."

"Not at all," Richard said heartily. "I'm pleased to meet you. I was hoping you'd have news about the other illegals."

Paul told him that eight people had been found and all were dead.

"That's too bad," Richard said. "I feel for those poor peasants trying to better themselves. Then to die such a horrible death in the desert! There was no sign of the smugglers or of Luana's sister, I suppose."

"No, I imagine they are long gone," Paul said. "Well, I had better be going. It was nice to meet you, sir."

"If we should want to get in contact with you, do you have a telephone?" Richard asked.

Paul hesitated a second. "No, but I'll be in touch — to see how Luana gets along."

A slight quiver ran through Joy's body. Paul had told them he had a telephone in his home and suggested he take Luana there so he could call the police. Could this man really be a *coyote* as Luana claimed? Had he planned to take Luana to his home and silence her forever?

It seemed preposterous. Paul was so nice — and thoughtful. She started to ask Skye if he remembered Paul saying he had a phone, but Richard was speaking.

"Luana told me this morning that she saw Paul with the smugglers of aliens on the Mexican border. That he's known as *La Vibora* in *coyote* circles.

"I wonder how wise I am to allow him to come here? He could be dangerous. The smugglers who left those poor illegals in the desert to die could be friends of his, or they may all be part of the same smuggling ring."

I won't mention the telephone, Joy thought suddenly. *Richard's obviously suspicious of Paul and will be watching him. Besides, we may never see Paul again.*

9

The next morning as Terry was coming down the stairs from his room, he met Mitzie coming up. He knew she had the room adjoining his, but he had not seen her since they first came to The Boulders.

The familiar resentment flared up as he caught sight of her. Terry thrust the feeling away. Keeping his eyes carefully on the steps, Terry passed her without a word.

Then he glanced down and saw his father standing on the landing a few steps below him.

"Good morning, son. I was coming up to see if you were going to sleep all day," Skye said lightly.

"Just being lazy," Terry said, moving down to stand on the step above him.

His dad smiled up at him. "I met a charming young lady in the dining room a few minutes ago who was asking about you. I believe she said her name was Nica. She asked permission to take you on a tour of The Boulders."

His dad punched Terry lightly on the shoulder. "Have fun! As for me, I have to work." With a grin, he bounded back down the stairs and headed down the hall.

Terry's steps lagged as they descended the curving stairway to the wide hall. "I wonder what Nica is up to," he muttered. Yesterday's tour was still vivid in his mind.

Conflicting emotions surged through his mind. He sensed that danger and recklessness were as intoxicating to Nica as wine. Part of him wanted to see her again, part shrank from it.

"Hi there, I've been waiting for you!" Nica greeted him as he came down the corridor. His heart leapt with pleasure that she had sought him out, but a quiver of alarm followed quickly on its heels at the expression on her face.

Nica glanced furtively up and down the hall, then lowered her voice. "Come with me and see what I've found!"

Terry swallowed nervously. "Maybe I had better get something to eat first."

"I've taken care of that! I haven't had breakfast either," Nica said, lifting a small cooler by its handle. "I had the cook put some goodies in this for us. Enough for both of us all day if we don't want to go the dining room to eat. As long as we're back for dinner this evening, no one will ask questions. And I told your father — and mother — I had plans for us today. So come on."

Terry heard a slight sound and looked up to see Mitzie standing silently on the landing above. Her blue eyes were wistful, and Terry read her mute appeal well. Mitzie wanted to be included!

An intoxicating exhilaration filled his heart. For once the popular Mitzie was being excluded instead of him!

When Nica noticed Mitzie on the landing, she smiled, waved, and quickly turned back to Terry. "She wants to go," she said softly, "but we don't need a baby trailing us around. Come on."

With a small, triumphant grin, Terry ignored Mitzie. Taking the small cooler from Nica, Terry followed her a short way down the hall to a stairway. Spiraling upward, it came out into a secluded little garden.

Under the glossy-leafed shade of a lemon tree, Terry saw two large, brightly-cushioned chairs and a small, white enameled table set among flowerbeds of brilliant flowers. A fountain sprayed a fine mist into the air before falling back into a bright yellow birdbath.

As they entered, a tiny, jeweled hummingbird darted down to dip its long bill into a bright blossom. Two rather drenched grey birds hopped from the fountain spray to the edge of the birdbath to preen their feathers.

Terry was surprised that Nica had brought him here. This quiet little hideaway would be a wonderful place to read, to be alone, but somehow he couldn't envision the restless-natured Nica even liking to read — or relax.

"Spread this on the table," Nica directed, removing a bright green-and-yellow-checked tablecloth from the cooler. He quickly complied. She laid a tempting meal out on the table: doughnuts, ham and cheese sandwiches on rye bread, pickles, potato chips, and deviled eggs. Her little cooler even produced disposable glasses, a quart of milk, and two Pepsis.

"Help yourself," Nica said as she handed Terry a paper plate and napkin.

Terry was ravenous so he didn't need a second invitation. As they settled down in the comfortable chairs and began to devour the food, Terry wondered if he had misjudged Nica. She was acting like a very ordinary girl today: spreading their picnic lunch like a hostess and obviously enjoying the antics of the birds who were enticed by the misty birdbath.

She even laughed out loud when a tiny

brown hummingbird dive-bombed another of his kind, just missing its glistening green head.

When they had finished their meal, Terry helped Nica gather up the remnants and put everything back in the cooler. Nica brushed the crumbs off into her hand and put them in a small trash container.

"Now for some music," Nica said. She walked over to a small cabinet tucked into a wall from which she took a cassette player and a plastic case of cassettes. "This is one of my favorites," she said as she inserted a tape and pressed the play button.

Music crashed from the recorder and Terry winced. Hard metal rock was not his idea of good music, especially at this ear-splitting, nerve-jangling volume. But after the initial shock, he tried to act as if he enjoyed it. After all, she didn't need to know that his father didn't allow rock music in the house. He didn't want her to think he wasn't as worldly wise as she.

As the music got wilder and wilder, Terry noticed uneasily that Nica seemed to change before his eyes. Her body began to writhe with the music, and her hands moved in jerky motion, beating time to the frenzied beat of the thundering music.

The song ended with a violent crash of

sound. The silence felt good to his ringing ears, but to his horror, Nica bounced up, took out the cassette, and put in another, clicking her fingers and contorting her body as if she were still hearing the music.

Nica whirled and jerked her body convulsively in time to the second tape. In spite of the booming on his tortured eardrums, Terry sat in fascinated awe. The whole unreal scene made him think of a home movie a friend of his father's had shown them once: a frenzied native dance, inspired by the weird and wild music of voodoo drums in the jungles of Africa.

When the cassette ended, Nica fell laughing into a chair. "That is such fun. I'm wild about that music! It causes my blood to boil and makes me crazy!"

Terry was silent. He wished he were bold enough to tell her he liked other music better.

Nica turned her green eyes upon him. "You don't like it, do you?" Her lips began to curl. "I had forgotten that your whole family is into religion. Real deep, my father said." She laughed suddenly, a trifle high as if she were keyed up and couldn't come down. "My dear old dad said it wouldn't hurt if a little of it rubbed off on me!" She laughed again, high and scornful.

70

Terry felt his face grow hot and tried to think of something to say. He had never been ashamed of his family or his faith in Jesus, but under Nica's scorn, he suddenly saw them in a different light. Obviously Nica — and her father — thought his family was odd and old-fashioned! It came as a decided shock.

"Well, why don't you say something?" Nica asked sarcastically. "Cat got your tongue?" Suddenly she jumped up. Her eyes were spitting green fire. "And I was going to show you what I discovered! Well, go back to your mother, Terry Teddy Bear. You aren't any fun!"

Stung to the core by the girl's scorn, Terry leaped to his feet and started for the door, his face as white as the lilies in a nearby flower bed.

He yanked open the door, but before he could step outside, Nica's long fingers were on his arm. Her eyes were dark green pools of pleading. "Terry, I don't know what got into me. Sometimes I do crazy things and say awful things. But I really don't mean them. Come on back and I'll show you what I found."

Terry's jaw set stubbornly. He tried to pull away.

"Look at me, Terry, please." Nica's voice

was soft and pleading. "Please say you for-give me. Please?"

Terry couldn't resist glancing around. Her pretty face was the picture of dejection and contrition.

"Oh, all right," Terry relented. "But if you play any more of that music, would you turn down the volume? My ears hurt."

"I'm going to show you my discovery," Nica said, her eyes dancing with excitement, ignoring his request.

Running to the small cabinet, she drew out a little packet filled with white powder and brought it over for his inspection.

"What is it?" Terry said uneasily. Nica seemed to tremble with a suppressed excite-ment.

"Snow," Nica breathed. "Did you ever try snow?"

"Snow?" Terry's stomach began to knot with dread.

The dimple in Nica's smooth cheek dis-appeared and her red lips drew back in scornful unbelief. "Don't tell me you don't know what 'snow' is! Where have you been all your life? Terry, you *are* an infant! Coke! Cocaine, if I have to spell it out for you!"

"Where-where did you get that?" Terry croaked through stiff lips.

Nica's arched brows lifted disdainfully.

"In the satanic worship room. I borrowed it this morning, and I have to put it back. But they won't miss a little. Do you know how to use it?"

"No! And I don't want to know how!" Terry said emphatically.

Nica's emerald eyes narrowed and turned cold. "You're the sissiest boy I ever saw! An utter wimp! I suppose your religious father told you all the dangers of drugs — like a good father should!" Contempt and loathing seethed in every line of her lovely face.

Terry's face paled under her sarcasm but the scorn in her eyes was reflected in his own clear blue ones. "Yes, my father — and Joy — both told me about drugs. And if yours didn't, they're very poor parents!"

Nica laughed — brittle and high. "Oh, yes, my mother told me about drugs and their horrors — while using alcohol both night and day! Oh, she tried to hide it — the short periods of time I was home — but she can't function without her booze!"

Nica laughed again, almost hysterically. "And Daddy! Oh yes, I hadn't been here two days before he gave me the little lecture about drugs, like the dutiful father he is!" Her laugh was derisive. "I could tell you some things about my saintly father that would knock your brains out — but I'm not going to. Why spill all the family secrets in one day? Some of the things that go on at his parties! Just trust me — his words are so much gravel rattling around in a tin can!"

"Even if your folks don't practice what they preach, you know it's dangerous to use drugs," Terry argued. "You could become addicted to drugs, like your mother is to alcohol."

Nica's face showed incredulity. "You are such an innocent infant! I've lived almost exclusively in boarding schools and summer camps most of my life, and you can buy almost anything at them. I've been sampling most illegal drugs since I was ten."

She laughed at Terry's astonishment. "Some of the kids I know spend all their allowance every month on drugs — or alcohol. What do you think I was kicked out of school for? Playing pranks on teachers? No! For drugs, that's what! Ice is my favorite, but cocaine isn't bad."

Nica's eyes narrowed into green slits. "Do I look like the addicts that parents and teachers insist you will become if you use a little drugs now and then?"

Terry shifted from one foot to the other. "I guess not," he said uncertainly.

"Just the idiots who get greedy get hooked on drugs," Nica said airily. "Just like the ones who guzzle alcohol instead of taking a little nip now and then."

She tilted her bewitching face to one side and the deep dimple slipped into place in her cheek. Her lips curved into a small conspiratorial smile. "I'm going to have a little snort of cocaine. Just one. You're welcome to join me."

She waited, the tiny smile still hovered on her sculptured lips; a reckless, dare-devil light glinted in her eyes.

"Well — I suppose a tiny bit wouldn't hurt," Terry conceded doubtfully. He felt light-headed, and his heart seemed to be trying to hammer its way out of his thin chest.

"Terry Windthorn, have you lost your mind!"

Both Terry and Nica whirled around. Standing just inside the doorway was Mitzie. Her softly rounded face was pale, but her eyes were flashing blue fire.

10

Fierce anger slashed through Terry. "Mitzie, how dare you follow and spy on us!"

But Mitzie wasn't intimidated. Her small, sturdy figure stood ramrod straight as she said scathingly, "It looks like someone should follow you around — both of you! I'm not very old, but I have more sense than to fry my brains with drugs!"

"Get lost!" Terry said furiously.

"Oh, I'm going," Mitzie said emphatically. "Straight to Daddy and tell him the crazy thing you're about to do!" Her eyes still blazing with anger, she turned and walked out.

"Catch her! Don't let her go tell!" Nica yelled in panic.

Both Terry and Nica raced to the doorway and nearly collided with each other. "Come back here," Terry ordered Mitzie's retreating back. When she didn't stop, he bounded down the steps after her with Nica close behind him.

Mitzie fled down the stairs, but the two

quickly overtook her before she reached the first landing. Terry hauled her to an abrupt stop.

Mitzie backed up against the stone wall and faced them defiantly.

Terry took a deep breath and tried to speak quietly. "Mitzie, there's no need to go blabbing to Dad. I'm not going to take any drugs."

Mitzie eyed him suspiciously. "Promise?"

"I promise."

"Well — okay," Mitzie said. "And I wasn't spying on you. Mother sent me to find you. Mom has to run into town, and invited all of us kids if we want to go. Daddy isn't going."

"We don't want to go, do we, Terry?" Nica said quickly.

Terry really would have liked to go, but he didn't want to appear a baby in Nica's eyes. "No, I'll stay here, too. You go ahead and go, Mitzie. And remember, you promised not to tell Dad about the drugs."

Mitzie stared at Terry a moment and then said seriously, "I won't tell. But remember what you promised." She waited for Terry's reluctant agreement before going on down the stairs.

"Your baby sister is concerned about her big brother," Nica said sarcastically, her pretty mouth curling unpleasantly.

"She's not my sister!"

"You sure minded her like she was your *big* sister," Nica said contemptuously.

"Did you want her to tattle on us?"

"If she's like most kids, she'll tattle anyway, regardless of what she promised!"

"Mitzie won't," Terry said emphatically. "When she makes a promise, she keeps it."

For a moment Nica stared at him. Then she suddenly dropped her eyes and started back up the stairs. "Come on, let's don't let her ruin our day."

Terry followed her reluctantly. Nica fascinated him, but at the same time she filled him with dread at what she might do next.

Nica went directly to the table in the room they'd left and picked up the small packet of white powder.

"Come on, I'll show you how to take a snort of snow," Nica said. Her eyes glowed strangely.

"You mean you're still going to use some of that?" Terry asked incredulously.

"Sure, why not? Are *you* afraid to?" She lifted her shapely chin and looked him full in the face.

Terry knew it was a challenge. He dropped his eyes. "I promised I wouldn't."

"A promise to a child! She pushed you into it! You certainly aren't obligated to keep a promise like that!"

Terry didn't meet her eyes but shook his head.

"That's a cop-out, Terry! You're afraid to! And you're hiding behind your little sister's skirts to keep from admitting you aren't man enough to try something new!"

Sudden anger rose in Terry. "You're right! I don't want to try drugs! I have more sense than that! You carry on about other people getting hooked and that you never will. That's what every drug addict from here to Kalamazoo said before they got hooked!"

Nica's eyes darkened and her face twisted in fury. "You make me sick! I called you Teddy Bear Terry and that's just what you are! Little sissy Terry! Go on and play dolls with your baby sister!"

She came close to Terry and stared into his face with flashing green eyes. Her voice was cold. "I was going to invite you to join me on a special adventure, but you'd be too scared!"

"Wh-what are you going to do?" Terry couldn't resist asking.

"I've always wanted to see what they do at a satanic worship meeting. I plan to sneak in and visit one in that room we saw as soon as I can find out when they're having one."

"H-how can you find out?"

"I'll find a way," Nica said archly. "And

you're not invited when I do, you little sissy-boy!"

Terry felt the color rising in his face and cringed under her scorn. He stood looking at Nica for a moment, then he walked away. Turning at the top of the stairs, he said seriously, "Satan worship isn't a game, Nica. It's evil." A shudder ran through him as he walked down the steps.

"Don't you dare squeal on me, Terry Windthorn," Nica screamed after him, "or I'll make you wish you hadn't!"

11

Terry was in such turmoil when he left Nica that he charged down the stone stairway without paying any attention to the way he went.

His body turned hot, then cold, as he realized that he had almost taken some cocaine. He knew the horrors of cocaine. One of his classmates — a wealthy boy who had never lacked for any luxury — had died of an overdose just a month before school let out. He hadn't known the boy well, but the boy had once offered him drugs, just as Nica had today.

And I would have tried some if Mitzie hadn't stopped me! His heart leapt painfully.

His life seemed utterly out of control. For several weeks now, he had fought his growing antagonism for Mitzie. Well, perhaps he hadn't really fought it, he decided.

"I suppose I want to hate her," he muttered into the passageway emptiness. "But I don't want the hate to rule me. I should be able to control my feelings. And just now I

81

almost let Nica coax and goad me into using drugs. Don't I have any backbone anymore?"

His head began to throb. Suddenly he stopped and looked around. How long had he been plunging through stone passageways? He should have arrived in the main part of the house before now. Where was he anyway?

The air felt stuffy and smelled musty, like no fresh air had come in for a long time. The hair on his neck prickled with apprehension. Was he lost? He heard no sound nor saw any sign of life.

He leaned against the cool wall and held his throbbing head in his hands for a moment, trying to think. "I'll just take the next stairs that go up," he decided. "That should bring me out into open air, at least."

He looked around. This was obviously a storage area. A door on his left stood open and contained a few broken crates, a peeled brown table with only two legs, and some cardboard cartons.

His heart began to beat more rapidly. Was he near the Satan worship room that Nica had shown him? A chill wind seemed to blow down his neck, and he quickly shrugged it off. A faltering prayer sprang into his heart. *Lord Jesus, please protect me.*

As he walked past several closed doors, he was sure that they looked familiar. Then, suddenly, he was standing at the door of the satanic worship room. He glanced furtively around, then reached for the doorknob, unable to resist another glance at what lay behind the heavy door. But this time, it was locked.

A surge of relief swept over him as he walked quickly on and turned the corner. Just ahead, a steep stone staircase climbed toward the ceiling. Hurrying to it, he went up in a few quick leaps. He wanted out of this place.

He didn't stop at the next floor. He found another stairway at the end of the hall and climbed the steep stairs to the top. Opening a heavy door, heat, like the blast of a furnace, struck him. As he stepped out, to his right was a large air-conditioning unit, humming away as it poured refrigerated air into the house below.

Terry crossed the smooth silvery roofing. He could feel the heat coming up through the soles of his athletic shoes. At the edge of the roof, he leaned over a low parapet and peered into a small courtyard. A pickup was parked there, but no one was in it.

The heat beating down on his bare head was intense, so he turned to leave, but a movement arrested his eyes. He stepped back and crouched down behind the low wall, his mouth open in surprise. The far wall was sliding silently apart. An old Volkswagen van slipped through the opening. The gap in the wall then slowly slid back into place and no evidence remained of a gate.

Terry lowered his head until he could see but not be very noticeable and waited.

Two Mexican men spilled from the doors of the van. One was a heavy, muscular man with a shaggy mustache; the other, whip-lean and rather good-looking except for too-long black hair.

While the lean man ran and opened a door in the building, barely in Terry's sight and to his right, the muscular Mexican opened the back door of the van and began to work at something inside the cargo area. The younger, slender Mexican came quickly back to the van, and the two began to drag a stretcher from the back of the van.

Terry gasped. There was a woman on the stretcher! He couldn't see her plainly, but she appeared young. One slim brown arm fell limply from the side of the litter; long black hair draped almost to the ground, covering most of her face. The men each took an end and started toward the building with the stretcher.

Terry leaned over the edge of the low parapet to see better. Suddenly, a strong hand covered his mouth while a powerful arm seized him, pinning his arms to his thin chest and lifting him bodily from the floor. Terry, petrified with shock and fear, let himself be carried back across the rooftop for a few steps.

Then his sense of self-preservation returned, and he began to kick and struggle violently. He tried to yell for help but the strong hand only tightened about his mouth; and the steel-like arm held his body so tightly it was painful to breathe. His captor shifted him to the side when Terry lashed out with a heel and struck him on the leg.

In a few strides the man was at the doorway of the stairs Terry had ascended a few minutes before. Moving down the stairs until they were well below the level of the roof, a voice hissed in his ear, "Be still, you little fool! Do you want to get yourself killed?"

Terry ceased struggling. The voice sounded familiar, but he couldn't remember whose it was.

"That's better," the voice said. "Now, I'm

going to release you, if you promise to keep still and do just as I tell you. Shake your head that you'll not scream if I turn you loose."

Terry remained still, trying desperately to think who held him prisoner.

The man shook him roughly. "I've no time to play games with you! You're in real danger if you're found here. Quick, give me your promise you won't scream, and I'll let you go."

Terry nodded his head.

He drew in a deep breath when the steely grip released him and turned to face his captor. Paul Tanner stood there, dressed in faded jeans, worn blue shirt, and athletic shoes. His black eyes were hard and his face looked grim.

"P-Paul," Terry stuttered, "w-what are you doing in Nica's house?"

Paul laid a hard finger on Terry's lips and said softly, "Keep your voice to a whisper!" A frown creased his high forehead. "I can't tell you why I'm here, and you must promise not to tell anyone you saw me."

"B-but I can't do that!"

Paul's hand snared Terry's arm so tightly he winced. His obsidian eyes flashed, and his voice was rough with anger. "Don't you realize you've stumbled into something you have no business meddling with? If you don't go now and keep your mouth absolutely shut about me — and what you saw just now in the courtyard — that girl out there has no more chance to live than a snowball has on that rooftop!"

Terry stared at him in disbelief.

Paul shook his arm roughly. "Don't you understand? Those men are going to kill that girl! And if you don't get yourself back down to where you belong and keep your mouth shut, you could be responsible for her death!"

"B-but I'll go tell my dad and Mr. Borders. They'll help her."

"No! There isn't time. And they'd probably ruin everything. Now, promise to get out of here and not to tell a word of this! If you don't, I'm going to have to tie you up and leave you here. What's it to be?"

"I-I'll promise," Terry said quickly.

"Go then! And remember — if you tell anyone about this, you could cause an innocent girl to die!"

Terry's blue eyes were wide and frightened as they locked on Paul's face.

"Go! Run! Get out of here! And if you come back, you'll wish you hadn't!" Paul said harshly, giving him a quick shove. His face was a hard, implacable mask.

Terry scrambled down the steps and didn't look back. Fear nipped at his heels and drenched his body in cold sweat. When he reached the next floor, Terry left the stairs and ran down a hall, putting as much space as he could between him and Paul Tanner.

Near the end of the hallway, Terry looked into an open doorway and saw a large bed and other furnishings, all draped with dust covers. Obviously, he was in an unused part of the house, but at least he was back in the house proper.

A winding set of carpeted stairs descended to his right and Terry started down them, almost colliding with the maid who had put his things away the evening before. Relief flooded through him at seeing another human being.

"I-I seem to be lost," Terry said, surprised that his voice sounded almost normal.

"You are quite a ways from your room," Margie declared. "At the foot of these stairs, turn to the left. Then turn right at the next hall. Your room is at the end of that hall and up the stairs."

A few minutes later, Terry closed his bedroom door behind him and lay down on his bed. He stared at the ceiling. What should he do? Could he trust Paul? The girl did seem to be a prisoner. Could she be Luana's missing sister? His heart missed a beat. If so, the smugglers were probably right here at The Boulders! Maybe they were the Mexican men who carried the stretcher!

He sat up abruptly. The smugglers had left nine people on the desert to die a tortured death from thirst and heat. Death by treachery was what the *coyotes* had given eight of those poor people in return for their money.

He jumped from the bed and headed for the door. He must tell Mr. Borders and his father about Paul — and the girl he had seen lying lifeless on that stretcher! His hand on the door, he hesitated. Paul's words flashed vividly in his mind:

"Those men are going to kill that girl! And if you don't get yourself back down to where you belong and keep your mouth shut, you could be responsible for her death!"

Terry went back and sat down in a chair. His head was reeling. What should he do? Was Paul going to try to save the girl? Or — his heart gave a terrible lurch — was Paul a *coyote*, like Luana declared, and was the helpless girl in the courtyard in extreme danger from Paul, rather than the two Mexicans?

Terry jumped up and paced the floor, What should he do?

Suddenly, he could stand the four walls of his room no longer. He jerked the door open and walked swiftly down the stairs and down a hall to the spacious, bright, front entry room.

No one was there but Luis the houseboy. Terry asked if he knew where Mr. Borders or his dad were.

"Yes," the young man answered with a wide smile. "They are in Mr. Borders' study. I just took them some refreshment."

On slightly unsteady legs Terry followed Luis's directions and found the study. He tapped lightly and Mr. Borders' voice called, "Come in."

Skye was holding an old book in his hand when Terry entered. "I thought you were with Nica," he said.

"I-we-I decided to come back down here," Terry said lamely. His heart was hammering and his mouth felt as dry as the desert sand. He still didn't know if he should break his promise to Paul. His father's eyes were intent upon him. "Is something wrong?"

To Terry's relief, the phone shrilled out. Their host picked it up. "Yes?"

Terry saw Richard's jaw tighten and his

lips went thin and white. "Find them," he ordered brusquely. "Get everyone available and find them and bring them to me! They couldn't have gotten far!"

Richard slammed the receiver down. His grey eyes looked murderous.

"What's wrong?" Skye asked.

Mr. Borders took a deep breath and looked at Skye without answering. He walked the length of the room and back and then said abruptly, "My men found Luana's sister wandering in the desert a short while ago and brought her here. She apparently escaped from the smugglers. But someone just now jumped my men and kidnapped her.

"He escaped in the old van that belongs to one of my men," Mr. Borders continued. "There's one thing in our favor though. That old rattletrap Volkswagen isn't a race-car, and I understand the motor has an ornery habit of quitting when it gets hot. They should be stranded somewhere soon, just waiting for my men to scoop them up."

His eyes narrowed in anger. "If this doesn't beat all! That girl kidnapped right out of my house!"

Before Skye could say anything, Terry spoke in a choked voice. "Paul Tanner kidnapped her. I saw him just a little while ago

— on the roof of your house. He said the men were going to kill her." He swallowed convulsively. "He made me promise not to tell anyone about it!"

His agonized eyes went to his father. "I didn't know what to do! Paul said I would be responsible for her death if I told anyone!" He began to tremble. "And now Paul may k-kill her."

Skye came swiftly to his side. "Terry, it'll be okay. You've told us now and that's a help. At least we know who took the girl. And we don't know that Paul will kill her."

"There's every possibility that he will," Richard said grimly. "We can be pretty sure now that he is part of a smuggling ring. Conchita is the only one who can identify the smugglers."

His eyes blazed with fury. "Except for Luana, of course. She is also in grave danger." He struck his fist violently into his other palm. "We've got to find that cur! And when we find him, I'll not be responsible for my actions!"

12

Richard picked up the phone. "I'll call my friend who has charge of the case." Dialing a number, he waited, drumming his fingers impatiently on the table.

"Bob?" he said suddenly. "I've some pretty bad news." He tersely narrated the story in an angry voice. A few minutes later he hung up and spoke in disgust. "I had a feeling about that Paul Tanner! Do you know what I have just learned? Bob has had his men checking up on my supposed-to-be-neighbor. No one by that name lives near here!"

"You mean he's a complete fraud?" Skye exclaimed.

"Absolutely! The name must be an alias. Also, no one of his description has acreage or even rents a house anywhere around here!"

"I'm sorry," Skye said. "I guess I'm the guilty one for believing his story and letting him come in here. Last night I suddenly recalled that he had told us he had a telephone and then told you he didn't."

"Don't worry about it," Richard said. "At least we know now. I'm going to Luana's room and tell her about her sister."

"Is that necessary yet?" Skye asked. "Perhaps he will be caught quickly, and Luana can be saved the grief of this newest development. The poor girl's been through a lot."

"I think she should know in case Paul tries to contact her with some story so he can get his claws on her, too. He's a pretty convincing guy."

Later in the day a tall, almost gaunt, middle-aged man appeared with two muscular young men — all well-dressed in lightweight summer suits. The Windthorns were called to the study to meet Bob Lawson, Richard's friend, who was conducting the investigation into the smuggling ring.

Terry was surprised to see Nica there, sitting in a chair near the window. She ignored him — and Mitzie — but smiled at Joy and Skye.

After the introductions, Bob Lawson launched right into his purpose at The Boulders. "I want to hear everyone's account of his or her involvement with this girl, Luana, and Paul Tanner. You first," he said to Terry. "I want you to tell me everything that happened and everything you saw. Don't leave out any detail."

Terry felt as if the tall man's bleak, greenish eyes were boring right into his brain. Avoiding those probing eyes, Terry told about leaving Nica in the patio — although he said nothing of what had happened while he was with Veronica — how he became lost and ended up on the roof where he was captured by Paul and carried into the stairway.

Mr. Lawson asked him to repeat what happened on the rooftop and his conversation with Paul, going over it carefully with him to be sure of every detail. He asked minute questions about everything: descriptions of Paul, the girl, and the van. One of his men took extensive notes, while the other stood by, silent but alert and watchful.

Then he questioned Skye, Joy, and Mitzie just as thoroughly about their part in finding the old Mexican and Luana before coming to The Boulders.

"Now, after I see where Paul Tanner abducted the girl, I must talk to Luana," he said when they had all told their stories to his satisfaction.

"Luana speaks no English," Skye said.

"That's no problem," Mr. Lawson said shortly. "I speak Spanish fluently."

"May I go with you?" Joy asked. "Luana is very timid and frightened of strangers."

"Certainly," Lawson said, "but I would like to do the talking, please. And let her give her own answers."

"Now," Bob's eyes pierced Terry, "I want you to take me to the rooftop where you were when you saw the girl, and then Richard can lead us down into the court-yard where the kidnapping took place."

"Can I go too, Daddy?" Nica spoke for the first time. "This is so exciting!"

Terry saw her father's frown disappear as Nica came over, slipped her hand into his, and looked up at him pleadingly. "Sure, sure!" He looked away from Nica's de-lighted face. "Perhaps the rest of you would like to go, too. This is quite an interesting old house."

Richard acted as a guide as everyone trooped after him. But Terry didn't think that Bob Lawson was too pleased that the others were invited.

When they entered the storage area of the mansion, Skye asked wonderingly, "what would anyone ever need with all this storage area? It's almost as big as a warehouse."

"You're right," Richard said. "It was a warehouse of sorts. The man who built this place was an extremely wealthy collector of fine art from around the world. Rare and beautiful wood carvings and jade treasures.

All kinds of art, even rugs and paintings were stored here until they were displayed and sold. He made a fortune in this place — to add to his already fabulous wealth.

"I bought The Boulders a little while after I met Monica." His face clouded briefly and he said softly, "Monica and I were very happy here for several years."

"Is this the place, Terry?" Bob suddenly spoke up briskly. The party had come out onto the rooftop.

"Yes," Terry said slowly. "There's the air-conditioner over to the right." He moved over to the low wall and looked down on the small courtyard. "That pickup was parked there, too. Yes, this has to be it."

He turned around. "And I was about here when Paul grabbed me and carried me back down into the stairway we just came up."

Bob Lawson walked to the edge of the parapet and looked down. "The van came in the gate down there and the men carried her into that door on the right?"

Terry turned back and said quickly, "The van didn't come through a gate. The wall just sorta slid apart and the van came through."

Bob spoke shortly. "The sun must have blinded you, son. There is a gate. Not real plain, but it's there."

"I see one now," Terry said in bewilderment. "But I'm sure there wasn't one there this morning. This must not be the right place."

Richard moved up beside Terry and looked down. "It has to be the place, Terry," he said. "There isn't another courtyard or storage area like this one. If you'll notice, there is a layer of something on the gate to make it look like the blocks of the wall. And it slides to one side, like you said. This is the only entrance into the storage area so it has to be the place."

"I-I suppose so. But-but I was sure there wasn't a gate in the wall at all; it just-just slid apart."

Bob Lawson turned abruptly toward the stairs. "Show us the way to the courtyard, Richard."

The courtyard was ringed in small storage rooms, all empty, except one which contained a couple of sacks of grain and a few bales of hay.

"I have a horse that I board out on a nearby ranch," their host explained. "When the weather is cool enough, I have him brought over for a day or two now and then because I enjoy riding. In the winter, our Arizona desert is a very pleasant place to ride."

When Terry walked over to the gate and studied it, Richard followed him. "See," he said, tracing the outline of a rock with his finger, "the covering on the gate looks identical to the rock of the wall it fits into. That's what had you confused, I'm sure."

He laughed lightly. "I'm wondering if the man who built this place was a smuggler of some sort. This gate is very hard to see from the outside, and there is a hard-topped road that runs next to the wall all around the outside of it. So no tracks of a vehicle coming in here could be seen. Pretty sharp, I think."

Suddenly he sobered and spoke softly, "Have you and Veronica had an argument of some kind? You two don't seem to be speaking this afternoon."

Terry felt the blood rushing to his face. "Yeah. I-I think she feels I'm a little too young to be much fun," he said lamely.

"Aw, Terry, I really don't," a husky voice said at his elbow. "Let's make up, okay?" Nica's smile deepened until her stunning dimple showed.

"All right," Terry said. It was hard to stay mad at Veronica. Her smile seemed to wash away any feelings of anger or resentment like a terry towel absorbing the water in a dish.

As her father moved away, a smile of approval on his lips, Nica leaned over and whispered, "I want to make up with you but that doesn't include your little sister. I can't stand a sneaky spy."

"I can't stand her either," Terry said. "And stop calling her my sister!"

13

When they returned to the main part of the house, Richard suggested that only Bob Lawson, Joy, and Terry go in to see Luana, so as not to frighten her. "She wanted to talk to you, Terry, since you actually saw her sister," he said.

However, Bob insisted on taking Larry, the young man who took notes for him.

As she followed the others, Joy wondered about Bob's two companions. She had never heard either of them speak. Larry, the shorter one, followed Bob about, scratching furiously on a pad most of the time. Bill, remote and unsmiling — though his eyes seemed to miss nothing — was never far from Bob.

Luana was sitting in a chair when they entered. As soon as she saw Terry, she jumped to her feet and caught him by the arm, talking wildly in Spanish. Terry backed away in alarm. Joy laid a gentle hand on Luana's shoulder, explaining that Terry couldn't speak Spanish. "I'll translate for you," she said.

So Terry told her quickly about his brief look at Conchita and that Richard had said she was asleep from a sedative his men had given her to make her sleep after her ordeal.

"Tell me about that terrible man, Paul Tanner, kidnapping her!" Luana demanded, with Joy translating.

"I didn't actually see him kidnap her," Terry said. He went on to relate quickly how Paul had captured him and carried him into the stairway, but Joy was fully aware that Bob Lawson was impatiently waiting to talk to Luana and staring holes in Terry as he talked.

"That man, I hate him!" Luana said bitterly. "I hope he dies a thousand deaths for his part in killing those other poor people — and now he will kill my sister!" She began to cry hysterically.

"That's enough of that!" Bob said sharply in Spanish. "It doesn't help to fall all to pieces."

His harsh words shocked Luana into silence; she twisted her hands together in suppressed anguish.

Joy explained gently that Bob Lawson was going to help find her sister, and Luana must help him by answering his questions.

Very subdued now, Luana sat with downcast, frightened eyes, but she nodded her head when Joy asked if she would cooperate.

"Please tell me exactly what happened from the time you decided to come to the United States," Bob Lawson said. "Whom you contacted to bring you into the United States — everything."

When she came to the part of her story about crossing over the border, Lawson interrupted her. "What did you each bring over with you?"

"Only a little bag of clothes, a little food, a plastic bleach bottle that the *coyotes* gave us."

"What was in it?"

"The *coyotes* said it was water but ordered us not to drink any until we got to the meeting place across the border. They said it wasn't far."

"Who met you across the border? Was it Paul Tanner?"

"No, I only saw him with the *coyotes* in Sonoita. A big man met us in a Jeep. He collected all the jugs from us. He said water was scarce, and he would carry the water so everyone would get an equal share."

"Are you sure the plastic jugs contained water?"

Luana considered. "*Si,* it sloshed like water. However, we did not drink from the bottles. The man gave us each a drink before he drove away, but it came from a large can in the Jeep."

Bob studied Luana's face before going on. "When did the guides leave you?"

"Not until a couple of hours later. The man came back in the Jeep. When the two *coyotes* jumped in, they drove away with my sister, Conchita."

"And they left you no water?"

"Only one small bottle which they gave to me because my sister begged them to take me with them, too."

"Didn't any of the men try to overpower the smugglers and take the water — or the vehicle?"

"Some of the men were looking very angry so the big man in the Jeep pulled out a gun. No one wanted to argue with that!"

"Did you think the *coyotes* would come back for you?"

"We hoped they would bring us water. They told us which way to start walking and said they would soon return and let us drink some of the water."

"Why didn't you bring your own water with you?"

Luana's face grimaced with pain. "We gave them our money because we thought we could trust them. They promised to bring food and water for everyone." Her voice broke. "And they never told us what the desert could do to us."

She began to sob. "I saw them b-begin to d-die, one by one. I-I didn't walk as fast as the others so I got behind. Then I no longer could find them."

"How long were you in the desert?"

"Two . . . three days, I think. After a while, the sun seemed to make us crazy, so I'm not sure." A shudder shook her body. "I never knew such thirst, and my body was on fire. I was in so much pain I wanted to die."

"Why did you live and the others didn't?"

Luana swallowed hard. "I remembered from somewhere that cactus could keep one alive in the desert. So even though I got stickers in my hands and mouth, I tore one open and chewed it." She shuddered. "The pulp was bitter — but it was wet.

"Also, when I finally came across some of the others who were already dead, I saw they had taken off most of their clothes — trying to cool off. That was not wise."

A long tremor shook her slim body. "I cannot close my eyes without seeing those poor dead people. But if the rain had not come when it did, I would also be dead, I think."

Tears ran down her cheeks. "And if these kind people had not come to help me."

Joy squeezed her arm and smiled at her.

Bob asked a few more questions, then he and his secretary left abruptly.

Luana sat still for a moment after they left, then looked up at Joy. "I do not like that man. He is-is not kind."

Joy patted her hand. "He is rather grouchy acting, but he's trying hard to rescue your sister from Paul Tanner."

"I know." Suddenly her dark eyes blazed with wrath. "If I could get my hands on Paul Tanner, I would claw his eyes out!" Tears began to run in streams off her brown cheeks. "He will kill my sister and I hate him! Hate him!"

"There, there," Joy soothed Luana, holding her in a tight hug. "You'll just make yourself sick if you go on like this. Hate is like a poison. It does more harm to the one who hates than to the one who is hated."

"I don't care! I do hate him — with all my heart!"

Joy knelt by the side of Luana's chair and looked up into her wet eyes. "Luana, do you know Jesus?"

Luana stared at Joy in astonishment. "I-I think so. Why do you ask?"

"Because right now there's no one who

can help us like Jesus can. Hating doesn't help but praying can. But if we hold on to hate, God can't do a lot for us."

Luana looked at Joy intently. "I've said all the prayers I know and none of them have helped."

"Just saying memorized prayers isn't really praying, Luana. You need Jesus as your Friend and Savior so you can talk to Him and expect answers."

Luana was very quiet for a moment as she searched Joy's face. Then she said slowly, "I know now what you are. I knew you — and your husband, too — were different. Only one person I ever knew talked like you. She taught a Bible school for children in our village a long time ago. Mary was her name."

Her voice softened. "The mother of Jesus was named Mary. I know she would have been proud that that woman had her name. Mary! She had so much love! Even when we kids were bad."

"And she told you about Jesus?" Joy asked.

"*Si*. She told us that all people are sinners and that even we children needed to know Jesus as our Savior."

"Did you invite Jesus to be your Savior and Lord during the Bible school?" Joy gently probed.

A look of wistful yearning crossed Luana's face and she shook her head. "No, my mother would not let me go back. I never learned how it was done."

"God's still waiting for you to come to Him. Just ask Jesus to forgive you for all your sins. Thank Him for dying on the cross for your sins, for rising from the grave to give us eternal life, and invite Him into your life."

"Right now?" Luana said.

"Why not?" Joy said.

"I do not know how to pray. I do not know how to make prayers like you are talking about."

"Praying is just talking to God, just like you're talking to me. I'll be glad to help you pray, if you would like me to."

"Then I would have what you and my Bible school teacher had?"

"Yes." Joy smiled. "And Jesus will wash all the sin and hate from your heart and fill it with love and joy and peace."

A tiny frown appeared between Luana's darkly arched brows. "He would wash all the hate out of my heart?"

"Yes," Joy assured her. "Hate is sin so He takes it out of our hearts."

Luana's jaw set stubbornly. "I could never forgive Paul Tanner and those other *coyotes* for what they did to those poor people. You would hate Paul, too, if he had your Terry or Mitzie and was going to torture them!"

"You are right, Luana. Unless God helped me, I would hate them. But God could take it out of my life, if I'd let Him."

"No-no! I do not want to stop hating Paul and those other *coyotes*. As long as I am angry at them, I do not feel the pain so bad."

"But Jesus wants to take away that pain — not by hate but by love."

"Not now," Luana said, turning her face away from Joy. "I-I'm not ready to do this yet."

Joy stood to her feet and touched Luana on the arm lightly, "It is your decision to make, Luana. We'll be praying for you."

Signaling Terry to come with her, Joy went out the door.

"What was that all about?" Terry asked as they went down the hall.

Joy told him briefly. "Luana needs someone to blame right now, I think, so she isn't ready to let loose of her hatred for Paul Tanner and the other smugglers. What she doesn't understand is that hate and resentment are powerful emotions. Hate destroys the one who hates. It can make the person's body sick, but worse yet, it makes the person's mind sick. No one can afford the luxury of hating."

Joy was so intent on her own musings that she didn't notice the catch in Terry's voice as he asked, "But how can a person keep from hating someone that hurts them?"

"A person can't without God's help."

"But-but if a person hates someone, God wouldn't even listen to him, would he?"

Joy suddenly stopped and looked down at her stepson. "Have you got a problem with hating someone, Terry?"

Terry looked away and said quickly, "Not me. I was just curious." He started to walk away.

"Terry, wait," Joy said. As he turned back to her, she reached out and put her hand under his chin, turning his reluctant eyes up to hers.

"Terry," Joy said slowly, "I have been worried about you lately. I know you are going through a difficult time right now."

Terry began to stutter a denial but Joy stopped him. "It may only be that you are in the transition period between childhood and adulthood. That can be a confusing and difficult time — especially for a boy. But you have been cross lately and at times, even sullen with Skye and me, as well as hateful to Mitzie. Couldn't we talk about it?"

Terry hung his head and said nothing.

"I'm not trying to scold you, Terry. It's just that I'm concerned about you. And especially about your actions toward your sister."

Terry stiffened and before he could stop himself, he blurted out, "She isn't my sister!"

Joy was shocked into silence for a moment, then said in a horrified voice, "What an awful thing to say! Of course Mitzie is your sister!"

"She isn't my sister!" he shouted. "Just because you married my father doesn't make her my sister!"

Skye stepped into the hall at that moment and heard Terry's last words. He stepped over to Terry and spoke sternly, "You will apologize this moment to your mother for shouting at her."

Terry wilted under his father's angry glare. "I-I'm sorry," he muttered.

"Now go to your room until you can act like a human being," Skye thundered.

Terry turned and ran down the hall and up to his room, sobbing like he had not done since he was a child of eight.

14

Luana was startled awake by a soft voice whispering urgently in her ear. "Wake up, Luana. I've come to take you to your sister." In the dimness of her room, Luana could not see who the person was, though the voice was a woman's. The words were in Spanish but with an American accent.

"Who are you?" Luana quavered.

"Shhhh," the soft voice whispered. "I'm a friend, and I'm going to take you to your sister. Get dressed quickly."

"Mr. Borders said I musn't go with anyone unless I tell him first," Luana said doubtfully, now fully awake.

"If you do not come quickly and without a sound, I will go away and you may never see your sister again," the voice whispered sharply.

"I'm coming," Luana said, sticking her toes into soft bedroom slippers, "but I have no clothes except the pajamas I have on and a robe."

"Come then, and do not make a sound. If

we meet anyone, tell them you were trying to find the kitchen to get some milk to drink, became lost, and I found you."

The figure stuck her head out of the door and looked both ways before reaching for Luana and drawing her out the door. As Luana was guided swiftly down the hall and down some stairs, she tried to see who her guide was, but the woman wore a robe with a hood drawn about her face.

Luana was quickly panting, exhausted, weak, and trembling as she was hurried down a series of stairways and short halls. Fright rose in her throat as they got farther and farther from her room and the hallway lights became dimmer and dimmer.

Finally, Luana gasped and said she must stop to rest. The woman reluctantly loosened her hold on Luana's arm. Glancing back down the hall, she whispered urgently, "Only for a minute. You'll have to sit on the floor."

Gratefully, Luana leaned against the wall and let herself slide to the floor. Her guide crouched down near her, alert and watchful. Resting her head against the wall, Luana spoke in a soft voice. "How do I know I can trust you? Maybe you are trying to kidnap me, like that Paul Tanner kidnapped my sister."

For a moment the woman at her side was

silent, then she whispered, "Here, does this belong to your sister?"

It was the soft silk scarf that her sister had brought with her from Mexico! Luana took the scarf in her fingers, then held its softness against her cheek.

"Your sister said you gave her this," the soft voice continued.

An overwhelming desire to hold her sister in her arms swept over Luana and she struggled to her feet. "I'm rested now. Please take me to my sister."

After a few more minutes of walking, a heavy wooden door loomed before them. Glancing around, the woman took a key from her pocket and opened the door. It swung toward them with a dull grating noise. The guide pulled her quickly out the door, then stopped for a moment to listen and look in every direction. "Don't make a sound," she whispered urgently.

They sped across the lawn, its soft green grass muffling their footsteps. The rumble of distant thunder broke the stillness of the sultry darkness. Even this late at night, Luana felt the uncomfortable heat.

Reaching a hedge near a wall, her guide drew Luana behind it and pulled her down on the ground next to the wall. The woman gripped her arm with tense fingers as they waited for several long moments. Suddenly Luana gasped as, almost noiselessly, a figure dropped to the ground beside them, then another.

The first figure spoke a few soft English words to her guide, who then whispered to Luana, "They are going to take you over the wall on a stretcher. Lie down as they direct you and be very quiet." She pointed to an object on the ground, barely visible in the murky light.

The first man took her arm and indicated she should lie down on the stretcher. He whispered something to the other man and he answered quietly. Luana stiffened and drew back. The second man's voice was only a whisper, but it sounded familiar — and it caused a tingle of fear to shudder down her back.

"Please lie down quickly," the soft voice of the woman whispered. "Please — quickly!"

"No, not until I know who that man is," Luana whispered, pointing to the second man. For a breathless moment, everyone seemed to freeze. Suddenly Luana's alarm erupted into panic and fear. Something was wrong!

Opening her mouth to scream, she felt a strong hand whip across her lips. Then steely hands were upon her body, lifting her and forcing her down upon the litter. She fought like a cougar but her efforts were futile.

A rag of some sort was stuffed in her mouth and secured with a band of cloth around her head. Her hands and feet were hastily tied and her body lashed to the stretcher. Although it was dark, the hands seemed to have eyes, as they moved swiftly and silently, strapping her to the litter.

Terror almost paralyzed her as she realized how helpless she was in the hands of the three. Tears of helplessness and fear ran down her face.

With a minimum of effort, her two captors — the woman had vanished without a word — raised her to the top of the wall on ropes. A third person waited at the top of a ladder to steady her while the other two men climbed up on the ropes.

There was almost no noise as they slid her stretcher down and put her in the back of a large, dark panel van. The ladder was folded down and placed beside her. One of the men jumped in the back with her, and she heard the other two get in the front and ease the doors closed.

The engine purred to life, and they began to roll silently away. Luana tried to think, but her mind seemed disjointed and jumbled. Only one thought surfaced clearly. *I wish I had let Joy pray with me. They are probably going to kill me, and I don't want to face God when I wouldn't accept His Son as my Savior.*

They had traveled for a while when she saw the man sitting near her raise his arm. She turned her head when he flipped on a small light in the side of the van. His face was in the shadows as he turned her head away from him and untied the cloth around her mouth.

When he pulled the rag from her mouth, she drew in a deep breath. She held still while he worked with the straps that bound her to the stretcher. Then, he untied her feet and helped her sit up.

"I hope you will be more comfortable now," he said in perfect Spanish. It was that familiar voice. Suddenly, before the man reached up and turned off the light, she saw his face. Paul Tanner!

Anger exploded in Luana's brain, driving out all fear. "What have you done with my sister, you — you viper!"

The man settled his lean form languidly against the wall before he chuckled softly. "My-my what a temper you have, Chiquita."

"You *are La Vibora*," she accused. "And you *can* speak Spanish!"

"Call me what you like, Chiquita," he laughed softly. "And yes, I do speak Spanish. It is my native language."

"What have you done with Conchita?" Luana demanded again.

"She is safe, and you shall see her soon."

"You are going to kill us both, aren't you? If you haven't already killed my sister!"

Suddenly the voice was no longer soft but cutting and harsh. "I have not killed your sister, and I do not plan to murder you. Now, please shut up and let me get some sleep. It's been a long night."

Not a minute later Luana heard deep, steady breathing and knew that Paul Tanner was asleep.

15

Luana was awakened the next morning by a soft knock on the door. For a moment she couldn't remember where she was. Her mind searched groggily in her memory until she sat up and looked around. Instantly, she was wide awake.

Paul Tanner had brought her into this house last night and locked her away in a room. "Do not try to escape," he had said. "There will be a guard right outside your door."

"Where is my sister?" Luana had said angrily. "You promised I could see her!"

"And you will, but not tonight. Now go to sleep," Paul had said irritably, before closing and locking the door. She had not thought she could sleep but, strangely, she had fallen asleep almost as soon as her head touched the clean, soft pillow.

The tap was repeated, breaking into her reverie. A key turned in the lock and a short, pleasantly plump, motherly-looking woman stepped into the room. Her round face, framed in black hair touched with grey and pulled into a loose bun at the nape of her neck, bespoke a Mexican heritage.

Crossing the room, her bright, black eyes gazed down at Luana. Her soft hand reached down and touched her cheek with a feather light touch.

"Call me Teresa," she said gently in Spanish. "Are you feeling better this morning?"

"*Si*," Luana said. "May I see my sister now?"

"Soon. Paul wishes to speak with you first. Put on your robe and come with me."

Her heart beating with both fear and trepidation, Luana slipped into her robe and soft shoes and followed Teresa across the room. As she passed a mirror, Luana smoothed her rumpled hair, wishing she had time to comb it. *That's ridiculous,* she scoffed at herself. *But,* she reasoned with herself, *even though I loath Paul Tanner, if I look my best, I can better stand up to him.*

"The bathroom is there," the woman said as they moved down a short hall. Pausing in the door she stood back for Luana to enter. "Clean towels and washcloths are on the rack. Also, I've laid out a new toothbrush, toothpaste, brush and comb over next to the wash basin. But please hurry and freshen up, Paul needs to be going. I'll wait for you."

What is this place? Luana wondered, as she quickly washed her face and hands and dried them on a soft towel. Evidently they were expecting her — or was this a place where captives were brought periodically?

Sudden anger flamed in her heart. *The comforts of this home are bought with money that poor, trusting, innocent Mexicans gave to this-this horrible man,* she fumed. *He and other coyotes took our money, then left us to die like dogs in the desert.*

The urgent soft voice interrupted her harsh thoughts. "Please come at once. Paul is waiting."

"As if I care!" Luana muttered angrily, "But I might as well get it over with!"

The short, motherly woman led Luana past a couple of doors into a bright kitchen. Luana's heart leaped in pleasure in spite of her inner turmoil. The cozy room was filled with Mexican flavor, bright and colorful.

Yellow walls and sink, brown refrigerator and stove, and glowing walnut cabinets. The round table was covered with flowered placemats, and bright yellow cushions rested on the seats of the chairs. Mexican baskets, colorful pottery vases, and dishes were used as decorations.

Then she forgot the room.

Tanner, sitting at the table drinking coffee, looked up and drawled in Spanish, "Well, Chiquita, you look ready to go out on the town. Is that the latest fashion?"

Glancing down at her pajamas and robe, Luana said scathingly, "When someone kidnaps a woman in the middle of the night, he can't expect her to be dressed for the city."

Luana moved quickly to the table. "I demand to see my sister! What have you done with her?"

Paul's grin quickly vanished, and his dark eyes became frosty. "Sit down, I want to talk to you," he said brusquely.

"I won't talk to you at all until you let me see my sister!"

A dangerous glint appeared in Paul's eyes. "You'll see your sister — but not before we have out little talk. Now sit down and behave yourself!"

Shifting his cold eyes beyond Luana, he spoke gently, "Mama, would you please fix Luana something to eat?"

"I don't want anything to eat until I see my sister! I . . ."

Luana felt Teresa's soft hand on her shoulder, but his mother's words were for Paul, in English. They sounded mildly reproving and then cajoling.

A slight flush rose in Paul's bronzed face, and he lowered his eyes to his plate. Luana wondered what his mother had said to him.

With a gentle squeeze, Teresa turned away. Over her shoulder she said in Spanish, "I'll fix your breakfast. Please tell Paul what he wants to know, and I promise you will see your sister as soon as breakfast is over."

Teresa came back and placed a cup of hot coffee in front of Luana and put the cream and sugar near. Then she moved away, and Luana could hear her bustling about behind her back.

Paul picked up his fork and finished his breakfast, ignoring her as if she didn't exist.

Luana creamed and sugared her coffee. It was strong and good. A large ceiling-fan hummed softly as it stirred the cool, air-conditioned air about the cozy kitchen.

In spite of the man sitting across from her — his face almost hidden in his newspaper now as he drank his coffee — the peacefulness of this room and gentleness of the motherly woman who obviously presided here seeped into Luana's spirit, and her anger died.

When Teresa set Luana's breakfast before her, Paul laid his paper aside and said almost civilly, "While you eat, could you please tell me about your trip into the United States?"

Teresa put a plate of yeasty cinnamon rolls on the table between them. She smiled at Luana and nodded her head, as if to say, "It's okay; go ahead and talk to him."

And Luana did. While he ate two rolls and she ate her own delicious breakfast of bacon and eggs, she told him everything she could remember. He ate the rolls abstractedly, seldom looking directly at her as she told her story.

But Paul — like Bob Lawson back at The Boulders — became instantly alert when she mentioned the plastic bottles the illegals had been given by the smugglers.

"You say the *coyotes* took the bottles from you?" he asked.

"*Si.*"

"They didn't return them?"

"No."

"Don't you think that was strange — that they didn't give the water bottles back to you, I mean?"

"*Si,* and some of the men were very angry. Only the gun of one of the *coyotes* kept the men from taking the water bottles by force." Suddenly Luana stopped. "But you are one of the smuggling ring, are you not? You should know all of this."

Paul studied her face for a moment, but she could see he was not thinking of her. He

124

ignored her question. "Could the plastic jugs have contained drugs?" he asked abruptly.

"Drugs?"

"*Si,* drugs. You know: cocaine, heroin, illegal drugs."

It was a new thought. Luana suddenly wondered if that was what Bob Lawson was concerned about. "You-you mean the *coyotes* had us carry illegal drugs for them?"

"It's something to consider." His dark eyes held hers with an intensity that was a little frightening.

Luana dropped her eyes, her heart pounding. "C-could that have been the reason the *coyotes* left us to d-die? They didn't want any witnesses?"

"It is possible," Paul said softly. "Ten bottles of cocaine would be worth a lot of money — much, much money."

"Then the money we paid the *coyotes* would have meant very little to them."

"*Si,* just chicken feed."

"But-but why do you ask me all these questions?" Luana said, genuinely puzzled. Her eyes searched the rugged face. "You must have known it all. I saw you with the *coyotes.* You kidnapped my sister — and now me."

Suddenly her voice rose. "Mr. Borders told me why you kidnapped Conchita! And that you would try to get me! He said you know we could identify you!"

A slow grin curled Paul's thin lips, but he said nothing.

The grin infuriated her. "What are you going to do with us? Murder us? Like you did those poor Mexicans out in the desert!"

Paul's low chuckle brought her to her feet, poised to run.

Paul rose languidly to his full height and stretched leisurely. A lock of straight, black hair fell over his forehead. "I'm going, Chiquita, so sit back down." His dark, dark eyes twinkled. "I was just thinking that anger becomes you. It puts fire in your eyes and color in your cheeks!"

With another infuriating chuckle, Paul rose and left the room, his boot heels clicking on the floor.

Luana wasn't aware that she was staring at the door where Paul had disappeared until Teresa spoke from beside her. "Don't pay any attention to him. He tries to act like he doesn't like girls, but I don't believe it for a minute."

Embarrassed that it appeared to his mother that she was flattered by his comment, Luana lifted her coffee cup and hoped her cheeks weren't still scarlet.

Teresa sat down in the chair Paul had just

vacated and said thoughtfully, "I wish my son would find a nice girl and settle down. I would like some grandchildren."

Lifting her hands in exasperation, she continued, "He is so secretive, that one! I worry about him. He comes and goes and I never know if he is safe or not."

Luana set her coffee cup down with a little click. This sweet little mother did not know her son was a smuggler — maybe even a drug dealer. Luana's eyes widened as she stared at Paul's mother.

A new thought came to her: Had someone else stolen the drugs Paul wanted, and was he trying to find out where they were and who had taken them? Was that why all the questions? She hoped she had told him nothing that would help him!

Paul's mother was speaking again, looking intently at Luana, "Paul is really a good boy. You mustn't ever think he isn't."

Luana almost gasped aloud. The poor deluded woman! Mothers never believed their sons capable of anything bad. Even if the evidence was right before their eyes!

Before she could stop herself, Luana said with asperity, "If he's so nice, why did he kidnap my sister and me? And what about the guard he had at my door to see that I didn't escape?"

"Paul didn't kidnap you and your sister! Where did you ever get that idea? He rescued you from wicked people who wanted to kill you both. Paul told me so!"

"Then we should be allowed to leave any time we want to."

Teresa looked distressed. "No — no. You can't do that! Paul left two guards to see that you don't leave and so no one can get to you. Don't you see? It is too dangerous for you to leave."

Two guards! I might have known, Luana thought.

"You promised me I could see my sister," Luana said.

"Of course! Come with me right now."

Teresa took Luana out the other side of the kitchen. "Her room is right down this hall, just past my own bedroom."

Her voice held mild disapproval as she added, "Conchita is probably still asleep. I think that girl would sleep all day if she didn't get hungry."

That sounds like Conchita all right, Luana assented silently.

Teresa moved ahead to the door. Taking a key from her apron pocket, Teresa inserted it and swung open the door. "Look who's here," she called cheerfully.

The bedroom curtains were drawn almost

closed, but Luana made out a figure slowly rolling over and then suddenly sitting upright. The figure catapulted from the bed and flung itself upon Luana. Joy surged over her as Conchita's strong young arms enveloped her.

Wrapping her hungry arms about her sister, Luana hugged her fiercely. Laughing and crying, the two clung to each other. *Whatever the future holds for us,* Luana thought in relief, *at least we are back together.*

16

Terry woke up very early the next morning. As he thought about the way he had mouthed-off to his mother about Mitzie, and his father's anger, he groaned and covered up his head. It would be fine with him if he just stopped existing on a day like this.

His father had been civil with him at dinner last night, but he could tell his dad was still extremely displeased with him. His stepmother kept glancing at him in a troubled way. *In fact, she looks that way a lot lately when she looks at me,* Terry thought with a pang.

If only Mitzie would just vanish from our lives forever! he thought angrily. *Then this overwhelming resentment would vanish from my heart. And I'd have my father back, all to myself,* he thought wistfully. Having Joy around was okay, "but I never asked for a sister," he muttered aloud. "And I don't want one now or ever! Especially perfect, pretty, smart Mitzie!" he declared derisively into the silence of the room.

"She's always showing me up, the little brat!" he said maliciously. "People are always bragging on her; it makes me sick to the stomach! I can't help it if I don't know how to get people to like me, like she does. It would serve her right to be in my shadow for a while, like I'm in hers all the time!"

Terry climbed out of bed and padded over to his dresser. Feeling around in a drawer, he pulled out an old drawstring cloth bag and drew out a tattered, brown stuffed dog. Hugging the small, ragged dog to his chest, he climbed back into bed.

"Sparky," he addressed the stuffed dog, "wouldn't Mitzie snicker if she knew I kept you around to cheer me up?"

Sudden tears blurred his eyes. He tried to stem their flow — he was much to old to cry like a baby — but they still poured down his face. His life was such a mess, and he seemed powerless to straighten it out. Everyone was mad at him.

He sobbed for a long while and when he finally fell asleep, Sparky — wet and rumpled — was cradled in his arms like a baby.

His room was bright with sunlight when he opened his eyes. Joy was standing over him, shaking him.

"Wha-what's the matter," Terry asked in

alarm when his eyes focused on his step-mother's face.

"Please get dressed at once. Bob Lawson wants to see everyone in the big foyer down-stairs," Joy said. "Someone has kidnapped Luana right out of her bed!"

"With Bob Lawson and his detectives in the house?" Terry asked in surprise.

"I'm afraid so," Joy said. "Poor Luana! She has been through so much and now this!"

When Terry walked into the mansion's big entry room a short while later, he saw that everyone — including a dozen or so ser-vants — was already there.

Bob Lawson stood up on a marble bench and called everyone around him. "I suppose by this time everyone knows we have had another kidnapping right here in this house. Did anyone see anything last night out of the ordinary, anything at all?"

"I found Robert, one of the other guards, lying on the ground," a burly man in uni-form said importantly. "He'd been chloro-formed."

"I know about that," Bob said. "And I want to talk to you later. Did anyone else see anything or hear anything?"

No one said a word.

Lawson's face was flinty and stern. "Let me tell you what I think happened. I believe that Paul Tanner kidnapped Luana just as he did her sister. And I'm beginning to wonder if he had an accomplice both times. One of you!"

His hard eyes searched each face. The silence in the room was absolute. Not a person moved or made the slightest sound.

Abruptly, Bob spoke into the silence. "If anyone here can recall anyone else acting strange or being somewhere they had no specific business, there will be a thousand dollar reward for you if you give me that information and it proves to be of value."

Flicking his eyes over the upturned faces around him, Lawson paused again. "That will be all. I'll be in Mr. Borders' study should anyone wish to speak with me."

Terry stood for a moment studying Bob Lawson. *I'd like to be a man like him*, he thought. *People look up to him and respect him — even fear him. I'll bet.*

He felt a hand on his arm and heard Joy's soft voice, "Go have some breakfast, Terry. I think everyone else has had theirs."

"Okay," he muttered as he moved away.

Skye came up and stood by Joy as Terry left the room. "I don't know what's getting into that boy lately," he said. "I can't get over how he yelled at you yesterday."

"I'm worried about him," Joy said. She hesitated and then said quickly, "Do you remember that little stuffed dog that Terry used to have?"

"You mean Sparky?" Skye asked, puzzled.

"Yes, Sparky. Remember how he slept with it when he was sick and having all those problems when I first met him — and you?"

"Sure, he wouldn't be separated from it. Why?"

"When I went to wake Terry a while ago, he had Sparky cradled in this arms, and he looked like he had been crying."

Alarm creased Skye's forehead. "I didn't even know he still had that old ragged stuffed dog! Maybe I was too rough on him yesterday. But even if he's upset, that's no excuse to yell at you."

"I've been uneasy about Terry ever since you and I married," Joy said. "Mostly about his relationship with Mitzie. I've mentioned my concern several times before, and I know you think I'm just expecting too much from them," she hastened to add when Skye's frown deepened. "I kept hoping they would grow to really care about each other like a sister and brother should. But it hasn't happened."

"I know," Skye said, "but we can't make

them love each other — or even like each other. Perhaps their personalities just clash."

"I've begun to feel there's a very real animosity in Terry's feeling for Mitzie," Joy said. "And I can't understand it. She has a knack for making friends. So why doesn't Terry like her?"

"She doesn't go out of her way to make Terry like her," Skye said shortly. His slate grey eyes darkened, and his jaw took on a stubborn look.

"Skye," Joy's eyes were beseeching, "please don't take that attitude. I've tried to discuss the children before, and you refuse to believe there's anything really wrong between them. Please — can't we talk about it?"

Skye's knuckles went white on the back of the chair he was behind. He took a deep breath and expelled it slowly. "I'm sorry, Joy. I guess I'd had my fill of problems with Terry before I met you. Perhaps I keep hoping if there *are* problems, they'll just go away."

Joy laid her hand on Skye's hand. Her gentle blue eyes were distressed. "I know the pain you went through with Terry before I met you, but I have the feeling this problem Terry has now is very real, too. And different. Terry just keeps all his feelings inside, letting them fester."

"Don't I know it!" Skye said, not quite meeting Joy's eyes. "But I've asked him before if there is a problem between him and Mitzie."

"I know," Joy said, "so have I and he just shrugged it off."

"Then what else can we do?"

"I don't know, but I think we should make it a matter of sincere prayer. If it's serious enough for Terry, who considers himself so grown-up, to cry about and to go to Sparky for comfort, it's serious."

For the first time Skye looked Joy in the eyes. "I've been worried, too. I know Terry hasn't been himself since your dad and his wife stayed with them."

A muscle jumped in Skye's jaw, and an angry glint appeared in his dark eyes. "I think something happened then. Your dad shows a marked preference for Mitzie and almost completely ignores Terry."

A pained look shadowed Joy's expressive face. "I know. It wasn't a good idea to let them stay with the children. I should have stayed with them myself." Her hand crept into his. "I just wanted to be with you, and we honestly thought the children would be fine with my folks."

Skye's face softened and he bent to kiss Joy. "I'm afraid I was the selfish one. I wanted my wife to be with me. I can't stand being away from you. And there shouldn't have been any problem."

"Of course we don't really know that there was a problem during that time. Neither Mitzie nor Terry said there was."

"But Terry wasn't the same when he came back," Skye said emphatically. "I knew it as soon as they joined us in Mexico — I just refused to admit it, I suppose."

"And it has to do with Mitzie," Joy added worriedly. "He can't speak civilly to her. He actually seems to hate her!"

"I have only half-heartedly tried to talk to Terry," Skye said. "I'll try to have a serious talk with him right now, and see if I can find out what's troubling the boy."

"I'm glad," Joy said. "Whether you realize it or not, Terry idolizes you. Let's pray that God will take care of this situation and work it out. He's not just our son, he's God's child, too, and right now, I think his heart is pretty far from the Lord."

Oblivious to the curious stare of Luis, the houseboy, Joy and Skye joined hands and prayed earnestly for Terry and Mitzie, then asked humbly for direction and wisdom for themselves.

But when Skye went to Terry's room to talk with his son, he found only Margie, the blonde maid, cleaning Terry's room. She had no idea where he was.

"I came directly here from the foyer," she said, "and your son didn't return to his room. If I see him, I'll tell him you're looking for him," she said.

Skye thanked her, told her he would be in his room, then headed for the stairs.

A voice suddenly called his name. Skye turned and saw Richard hurrying toward him down the hall. "Have you got a minute to talk, Skye?"

"Sure, Richard. What's wrong?"

Richard drew Skye into a small secluded alcove. He took a cushioned seat and waved Skye into its mate. Worry-lines were etched into his face.

"I can't believe this is happening right in my house, with all the security we have," Richard began. "It's a little scary. One gets to wondering if any of us are safe."

"I suppose I'm to blame for bringing Luana here," Skye said regretfully. "But I never thought. . . ."

"You did what was best," Richard interrupted. "I would have done the same thing. I certainly don't blame you for the kidnappings."

Richard looked away from Skye for a moment in deep thought, then said abruptly,

"But I am concerned for the safety of you and your family."

"Why would we be in danger?" Skye asked in surprise. "We don't know anything that the smugglers might be afraid of."

"You probably aren't in any danger," Richard said slowly, "but both Bob and I are afraid that in some way you or some of your family might get pulled into this."

"You think we should leave The Boulders?"

Richard reached out and squeezed Skye's forearm. "I hate like mischief to see you go, but maybe it would be best. For now. I just don't want to take the chance that your family might be placed in jeopardy. If you went over to Tucson and stayed a few days and did some sightseeing — there's a lot to see there — maybe this will get cleared up and you can come back."

"That's a good idea," Skye said. "And if things don't clear up here, we'll just head on home to Idaho."

"Give this a little time," urged Richard. "I want you back here soon if it's safe. Don't think I am trying to get rid of you. It's been a special treat having you!"

"I understand," Skye said, "and I have to admit that I'd begun to wonder if it was safe for Joy and the kids to be here. I expect it will be a relief to Mr. Lawson to have no strangers underfoot in an investigation like this."

"I'm considering sending Veronica away, too. I'll have some of the maids help you get packed," Richard said. "And I want you to have a good lunch with me before you leave; we'll make some plans for your return. I can't apologize enough for the fiasco this visit has been for you."

Borders' eyes crinkled at the corners. "I promise there'll be no kidnapping, mayhem, or smugglers next time! It'll be so dull, you may not want to come back!"

17

Terry went to the dining room, but he didn't sit down to eat. A slender young man in a white uniform was clearing off the dining table.

When the servant asked what he would like for breakfast, Terry asked if he might have some sausage in a roll or a biscuit and some juice to take with him. He had a sudden desire to visit the swimming pool alone, and it would be a pleasant place to eat.

While Skye had given Terry and Mitzie specific orders that they could not go in the swimming pool without an adult being present, his father hadn't said he couldn't visit the pool.

Carrying his breakfast in a zippered plastic bag, Terry detoured by the large, well-stocked library. He quickly located a book to take along and started to the pool. Then abruptly changed his mind. He decided to see the courtyard again where Paul Tanner had abducted Luana's sister.

He walked slowly, trying to recall exactly the way he had first gone. After many twists and turns up stairs and down passageways, Terry finally came to the storage area Nica had brought him to. When he passed the satanic cult meeting place, he hurried past it, around the corner, and up the stairs to the next floor. He turned to the right and followed the hall to its end.

He stood before the blank wall, puzzled and bewildered. "I know there should be a doorway here," he muttered. Standing still in front of the wall, he carefully retraced his steps in his mind. He had to be at the right place — and yet there was no door.

"Well, I must be wrong," he muttered in disgust. He started to turn away when something on the wall caught his eye. The wall light was not very bright, but as he bent forward, he saw a very small piece of red thread protruding from the wall. A little tingle of excitement trembled down his backbone.

He tugged at the thread and it came free. Tucking the thread in his billfold, Terry tried to think above his rapidly beating heart. Had there been a secret opening here the other day that he had stumbled onto before it was discovered and closed?

This was a rather isolated section of the

house and probably no one came here except for a specific reason. Maybe someone got careless because of that. Maybe even Mr. Borders didn't know about this opening!

He thought of the dark-draped room Nica had shown him and shuddered. If a satanic cult was having meetings here — worship meetings — what else might be happening? Frightened by the thought of such a cult, Terry was suddenly gripped by what it meant. *Lord Jesus, protect us from this evil. I'm sorry I haven't told my father. Keep me safe, Lord Jesus. Please!*

A rough voice spoke at his elbow, interrupting his prayer, and Terry jumped almost out of his skin. "What are you doing here?"

A dark-skinned, stern-faced man stood glowering at him.

Before Terry could get his wits back together enough to make an answer the man frowned darkly. "I'm sure Mr. Borders would not approve of his guests poking about every cranny of his house. What are you doing here?"

Then Terry recognized him. It was Bill, the black-headed, smooth-shaven detective who had come with Bob Lawson.

Terry tried twice before any words would

come. His insides were quaking from the suddenness of the man's appearance in the darkened hall. "I-I just wanted to look at the courtyard where Paul Tanner kidnapped Conchita," he stammered.

"It's back down the hall and to your right," Bill said. "Come, I'll show you."

Terry followed him back to the corner and down a hall. At the very end was a doorway. The detective opened the door and preceded Terry up a steep set of stairs, through a door and out onto the rooftop. Crossing the hot roof to the low parapet, Terry looked out into the courtyard. The same pickup was parked there, and two men were lounging in its shade.

Suddenly Terry wanted to get away from this place — and the unsmiling detective. "Tha-thank you for showing it to me," he murmured. "If you could just tell me how to get down to the pool, I'll be going."

Still unsmiling, Bill gave him terse instructions, and Terry hurried back across the rooftop and down the stairs. The man didn't follow him, so after a few steps, Terry slowed and looked around. *I guess I was wrong about where the courtyard was,* he thought. *This big old place is so sprawling and massive, it's hard to keep everything straight.*

Terry looked back. The detective was nowhere in sight, so he proceeded at a slower pace toward the pool. It took him a while — he got lost a couple of times and had to retrace his steps — but after a time he found the sliding glass doors to the pool.

The light from the fierce Arizona sun appeared coolly green through the green dome over the pool area. He crossed the smooth green and cream tiling to the water's edge and looked across to the boulder in the middle. The sound of water rippling over rocks and splashing gently into the pool was pleasant to his ears. A wave of homesickness for the forest and streams of Idaho — and Windthorn — swept over him.

"This is such a lovely spot," he said aloud, "I wonder why it isn't used more?" He stood there thinking aloud, "Veronica said she doesn't like this place, but I wish we had it at Windthorn. I'd sure use it!"

He'd often wished there was a pool at Windthorn. His father and Washington knew how to swim and could teach him if they had a pool. Washington had offered to drive him into town so he could take swimming lessons, but Terry was ashamed for anyone to see his skinny body and had refused.

But Mitzie could swim! Joy and Mitzie often went into town and swam on women's and girl's night at the local pool. Yet he was three years older than Mitzie and couldn't swim a stroke! She could do everything better than he could!

Suddenly he heard another sound, muffled and indistinct, but it sounded like a moan. Goosebumps rose on his skin and his knees suddenly felt rubbery. He stood still and let his eyes rove through the large pool area.

At first he didn't see anyone. Then he heard another moan and twisted around. A figure was curled up in a large beach chair. It was Nica — but a Nica he had never seen before, except that she was dressed in characteristic flashy colors. She was the picture of utter desolation — pasty-white skin, tangled, unkempt hair, and barefooted.

Terry recalled now that he had not seen Nica at the meeting Bob Lawson had called in the foyer a short time before.

He set his breakfast down on a table and approached Veronica slowly and warily. She didn't seem to even be aware of his presence. Her emerald eyes — not shaded with eye color today — stared dully out toward the boulder in the pool.

"Nica . . ."

As if in slow motion, Nica turned her green eyes toward him but no recognition registered there.

Fear, like a burly, balled fist, struck Terry in the pit of his stomach. "Nica, wh-what's wrong with you?"

Nica's ashen lips parted. She licked her dry lips, then said very slowly, as if it took extreme effort to speak, "I-saw-them-kill-it." Large tears rose in her eyes and ran slowly down her cheeks.

Licking her lips again, she swallowed hard, then spoke laboriously. "The-poor-little-thing. I-heard-it-cry. It-didn't-want-to-die."

A spasm shuddered through Veronica's slim body. Her head dropped and her arms hugged her stomach as if she were in pain. Her body heaved like waves of nausea were wracking her, but she didn't actually vomit.

Terry knelt down beside her. He suspected Nica had already rid her stomach of all food and liquid. Laying his hand on her shoulder, he said urgently. "I'd better get someone to help you. You're very sick."

Nica lifted her white face and gasped out, "They-they drank its blood!"

"What are you talking about?" Terry said. Shaking her shoulder, he spoke sharply, "Nica, I'm going to get your father!"

"No!" Nica's cold hand grabbed his hand in a death-like grip. Now recognition was there. "Terry, I'll hate you forever if you say a word of this to my father!"

For a moment her eyes flashed in the old way, then suddenly they were dull again and her face and body drooped. Her cold hand dropped from Terry's wrist.

Terry put his hand under her chin and raised her head. "Nica, have you been taking something, some snow — or something?"

A sudden giggle burst from Nica's lips. "Just a little snort or two." She sobered almost instantly and looked up at him. She spoke slowly but more alertly now, "I tried to take it back to the Satan worship place, but they had moved it. They must have missed the cocaine — or saw us snooping around."

"So you've been using the cocaine?"

"Just a little — now and then." Nica giggled again inanely.

"What were you talking about before?" Terry asked. "What did you see killed?"

"A little white dog." Nica shivered. "When I saw they had moved the worship place, I waited until it was real late last night, then I took a flashlight and tried to find out where they had set it up again.

"I'd decided to tell my father about the room, but I knew he wouldn't believe me if I couldn't show it to him."

"Did you find where they moved it to?"

Nica's voice trembled. "I-I wi-wish I hadn't. When I didn't find it in any of the rooms of the house, I had this queer feeling — like I knew where it would be."

"What do you mean?"

"It-it's hard to explain, but suddenly I just seemed to know that it would be set up down here at the pool."

She covered her face with her hands. "And I was right! When I got here, a-a meeting was going on. People in black, hooded robes were gathered around the edge of the pool, chanting."

"Right here?" Terry exclaimed, looking quickly around.

"Yes. But the sacrifice took place o-over on that-that rock in the middle of the pool."

"S-sacrifice?"

"Yes! A priest ki-killed the little white dog. Right over on that boulder. He caught the blood in a big cup, and everyone drank some of it. I saw them!"

"Nica," Terry said, as sternly as he could muster from a powder-dry mouth, "you were using drugs and you just thought you saw all of that. It was just a hallucination, caused by the drugs!"

"It wasn't a hallucination!" Veronica said angrily. He could see the dullness in her eyes diminishing. "I didn't use any drugs last night — not until after I-I saw that horrible sacrifice."

"Nica!" Terry scoffed, "I don't believe a word of this. It-it's too far out!"

Veronica slowly raised to her feet, weaving a little but steadying herself with one slim hand on the chair arm. "Let me tell you something that will really blow your mind, mister-know-it-all!"

Nica's eyes were glowing now with that reckless, intoxicated-with-danger green light that fascinated, yet frightened, Terry.

She leaned toward him and spoke clearly but softly. "When I saw the satanic priest raise the knife to kill that poor little dog, I almost screamed. Because suddenly I saw myself lying on that rock with a long, shining knife drawn back in a man's hand over me."

Nica's voice quickened and trembled; her eyes were no longer focused upon Terry. They appeared almost black . . . and glazed. "In the picture in my mind, I heard a scream, and the man lowered the knife."

Tears began to flow from Nica's eyes, and she collapsed back into the chair. Her voice sounded thin and unnatural as she finished her narrative. "Then I came back to myself and saw the rest of the ritual. I heard the cry of the pitiful little dog and all the rest of the gruesome thing."

"But don't you see," Terry reasoned, trying to ignore the hollow, nauseous feeling in his stomach, "the whole thing was your imagination working overtime."

"It was not!" Nica denied hotly.

"But you know you weren't on that boulder over there, about to be sacrificed!"

"I know that," Nica said, impatience edging her voice. "But, don't you remember how I said I didn't like this place — the pool, the rock, any part of it? That it gave me a weird feeling? When I said I was on that rock, I meant I was remembering something that really happened when I was very small."

Terry shook his head in disbelief, but she gripped his arm until he winced and said angrily, "I don't care if you believe me or not! I did remember something that almost happened to me. I was almost killed on that rock over there in the pool, as a satanic sacrifice!"

"Who stopped it then?"

Nica shook her head. "I don't remember. All I heard in that memory flashback was a woman's scream. That's all I recall."

Terry, feeling like a herd of elephants was trampling through his insides, looked away from Veronica's earnest white face. Could her incredible story be true? Preposterous! his logic shouted.

151

Suddenly he had a new thought and turned to Nica. "How did the satanic priest get over to the boulder out in the water?"

Nica's eyes narrowed and a slight pucker appeared between her arched eyebrows, as if she were trying to remember. "There was a long, heavy board laid from the edge of the pool to the boulder, like a little bridge."

"And who was the priest who sacrificed the little animal?"

Nica shook her head. "I don't know. They all wore hoods. All the lights were off. Just a few black candles lit the ritual."

"Yet you saw the little white dog clearly?"

"Yes, there was a candle on the altar he was lying on. And I could see the priest plainly, too, but not his face because he wore a hood, like the others."

"Did you recognize any voices?"

"The priest said something but it was very low. Even the chanting was kept very low, perhaps so it wouldn't attract attention in the rest of the house."

Terry searched Veronica's face. Her eyes were still dilated but she seemed utterly sincere. "Who was the priest who almost sacrificed you when you were real little?" He asked, unbelief still strong in his voice.

Nica lifted her chin slightly. "I wouldn't tell you if I remembered. Why should I tell you? You don't believe a word I've said anyway."

Feeling around in the chair behind her, Nica's hand came out curled around a small packet that Terry recognized. She slipped it into her pocket and tried to smooth her tumbled hair.

Rising to her feet somewhat shakily, Nica suddenly shook her finger in Terry's face. "Don't you tell a soul what I told you or I'll deny every word!!"

"I won't tell. No one would believe me anyway. And I didn't tell anyone before, either," Terry assured her. But he wasn't sure she even heard him as she turned and walked slowly away toward the sliding glass door.

Neither one of the young people saw the dark figure of a man standing motionless behind a large potted palm tree. After Terry turned away from the sliding doors and sat down, the intruder slipped through the sliding doors without a sound.

18

Luana was getting increasingly jittery. She and Conchita had been prisoners at Paul Tanner's house for three days. She had expected that she and her sister would be taken out and killed, but nothing at all had happened. The suspense was becoming intolerable.

What did Paul and his two guards want from them? Why was he waiting to get rid of them? Luana almost wished for anything to happen, just to end the impossible waiting.

She had tried to question the guards when they came into the house for meals. They both looked friendly enough but neither spoke Spanish. And Paul! When she questioned him, he only grinned that mocking smirk. She felt like slapping it off his face!

He did make small talk with Conchita at meal times and the other times he dropped in. But then, no man could ever resist Conchita for long. She brushed her dark, waist-length, curly hair daily, until its coppery highlights flashed like subdued fire.

When she curved her softly-molded lips into a coaxing smile and looked at a man through half-veiled, copper-flecked, slightly slanted, brown eyes, most men just melted.

The first day of their incarceration, Luana had scolded Conchita for flirting with Paul. "That man is part of the ring that tried to kill us all," she argued.

Conchita only laughed. "More reason I should try to make him like me. You would do well to do the same. Besides I like him!"

"You like all men!" Luana snorted.

"If I can charm one enough, I won't be going back to Mexico," Conchita flashed defiantly. "And I'd marry the baldest, fattest, ugliest man in the United States if it meant I could stay! After all, later I could divorce him and get me a handsome one. It's done much in America, I've heard."

"I doubt you'll be staying in the United States or going back to Mexico, either," Luana said tartly. "I suspect, unless we can escape, that we'll be dead soon."

"Mother Tanner says Paul would never harm us," Conchita said.

"A lot she knows what that outlaw son of hers will do!" Luana said scornfully. "Mothers always think their sons can do no wrong! She doesn't even know he's a *coyote!*"

"You're always saying Paul's one of the smugglers," Conchita said angrily. "How do you know he's a *coyote?*"

"Richard Borders, the man who owns The Boulders said he was! *Señor* Borders was very kind to me, and I believe him. He even sent his men to search for you. And found you, I might add, until Paul kidnapped you away from them! Don't you remember?"

"No, I don't remember. The last I recall is when Pascual gave me a cup of coffee and a sandwich. When I woke up, I was here."

"You can't remember anything at all?"

"No. I remember that when the *coyotes* left you all in the desert, I was worried about you. But Pascual said one of their partners was going to bring you water and food and take you where you could find work. Pascual wanted to marry me, but he was not an American so I refused," Conchita finished archly.

"Then your sweetheart drugged you and left you out in the desert to die," Luana said scornfully. "Mr. Borders' men found you wandering in the desert. Don't you remember that at all?"

Conchita shook her head. "No, I can remember nothing of that. When I woke up, I was here. And Mother Tanner has been very kind to me and so has Paul."

"Don't call that woman Mother Tanner," Luana said. "She's the mother of our enemy!"

"She's a good woman and kind to us," Conchita said stubbornly.

It's true that Teresa is good to us, Luana thought, as she stood at the window on the evening of the third day of their captivity, watching the hot desert wind flutter the listless leaves on the huge cottonwood tree.

I wonder where we are? Except for a closely supervised walk outside the little house — watched carefully by the two guards — twice a day, she and Conchita were not allowed to leave the house. A high wall, equipped with strong, locked metal gates, surrounded the place. The windows were all locked down tightly — Luana had tried them all. And a guard constantly stood near each of the only two doors of the house.

Luana could dimly hear cars moving along a graveled road occasionally. Through the gates, she had glimpsed a road and empty desert, with only a few dusty greasewood bushes, clumps of dried scanty weeds, grass, and cactus. A saguaro cactus, with its arms stretched upward mutely, showed in the distance. Since she saw no houses, she decided their prison must be somewhat isolated.

She jumped and spun around when a voice spoke behind her.

"Luana, I must talk with you." Paul, clothed in his usual faded dungarees and western shirt, stood unsmiling, observing her with dark, alert eyes. His athletic shoes had made no sound on the kitchen floor.

"Must you sneak up on me?" Luana demanded angrily.

A hard glint appeared in Paul's eyes. "Must you always be so unpleasant?"

Her retort was broken off by a quick wave of his sun-browned hand as he ordered, "Sit down, there are more important things today than exchanging insults."

Luana sat on the edge of a kitchen chair, her hands twisted in her lap. Something had happened to erase the mockery and foolishness from Paul's face. His strong jaw looked tight and grim. Suddenly she was afraid.

Paul drew up a chair, straddled it, and looked directly into Luana's eyes. "I want you to believe me. This is not a game we are playing. I have reason to believe there may be an effort to kidnap you and your sister."

"Kidnap us?" Luana said in disbelief. "Don't you mean rescue us? You are the kidnapper!"

A glint of anger leaped in Paul's eyes for a moment. His hands tightened on the chairback until his knuckles showed white. Then he took a deep breath and slowly relaxed his hands. The fire faded from his eyes, and his voice was level and deadly serious when he spoke.

"I know it may seem that way, but I'm telling you again that it isn't true. You must believe me when I say you would not have lived to leave that house!"

"I will never believe that kind Mr. Borders is a murderer!"

"I'm not saying your kind Mr. Borders is a murderer — or a smuggler — though it's probable that he is. All I know is that someone in that house planned to murder you — and Conchita."

"I do not believe you! Everyone was very kind to me there!"

Anger shone dangerously in Paul's eyes and he stood quickly to his feet, knocking the chair over. "You little fool!" he spat out. "We risked our necks to save you and your sister's lives and. . . ."

Spinning on his heel, he stalked to the door. For a moment he stood with his back to her, his hand on the doorknob. Then he swung back to survey her through cold, fury-filled eyes, though his voice was calm and emotionless. "If we are attacked, and you help them to kidnap you back, you probably will not live long enough to regret it."

19

The shrill of the telephone sounded from the living room on the other side of the door. Paul opened the door and went out. He left the door slightly ajar, and Luana slipped off her shoes and moved softly to the opening.

Paul was out of her line of vision but her keen ears picked up most of his words, spoken in Spanish. "Is that so? . . . I don't like it! . . . I know, I know, I have no choice! . . . Thanks for warning me. *Adios*."

Luana nimbly darted back to her shoes and slipped them on. She had no wish to be caught eavesdropping. But she needn't have bothered. Paul went out the living room door, slamming it behind him — with a bit more force than seemed necessary.

A minute later Luana saw Paul standing in the yard talking with one of the guards. She noticed idly that black clouds were piling up in the sky, and the winds had begun to whip the cottonwood branches. Every afternoon since they had been brought here clouds had boiled up and the hot winds had stirred up dust, but no rain had fallen. Teresa called it the monsoon season.

The sudden image of rain brought the vivid memory of the monsoon rain that had fallen on her when she lay lifeless on the desert. Without it, she would not have revived enough to call for help. She would have died like the others!

I wish it would rain now, she thought. Even though moisture would raise the humidity, making the heat even more unbearable, it would be pleasant to see rain falling. At least it was usually quite comfortable inside the house. But their walks outdoors were not pleasant, even in the early morning and late evening.

"I'll never like the sun again!" Luana declared vehemently. "It is a merciless, cruel monster that saps the moisture from your body and burns your skin to a crisp!"

"Yes, the Arizona sun does that," Teresa's amused voice spoke from the doorway. "But you should be here in the winter! It's lovely then! There's nothing like a winter in the Arizona desert to make you forgive Arizona for its summers."

Luana smiled at the plump little woman. It was hard not to love Teresa: sweet, gentle, good-smelling — most the time of yeasty baked goods or spicy Mexican food. Her only fault, as far as Luana could see, was her blind trust and love for her son.

Teresa's smile sobered as she continued to gaze at Luana. Luana wondered guiltily if Teresa could have read her mind. *Were my thoughts mirrored in my face?* she wondered.

Teresa crossed to Luana and laid her soft hand on her shoulder. "I shall miss you, Luana."

Fear filled Luana's heart. "What do you mean?"

Teresa's gentle dark eyes misted. "Paul said some men are coming to take you and your sister to safer quarters."

"Who are the men?" She didn't voice them, but terrible fears crowded in upon her. Had the time arrived? Had someone given Paul the signal to do away with Conchita and her at last?

"Don't be afraid, dear," Teresa said. She reached over and touched her soft lips to Luana's cheek. "Paul will see that no one harms you."

That will be the day! Luana thought. Anger helped to force back the terror that was knotting her stomach and drawing the strength from her limbs.

"Come," Teresa said. "They won't be here for a while, and I want a good meal in

163

your stomachs before you leave. You can help me prepare it."

As Luana cut up vegetables and pounded steak for Teresa, she thought in despair, *And to think that I was almost wishing for a change of any kind. Now I'd be willing to putter around in Teresa's kitchen and pretend I would never have to leave it.*

Conchita came into the kitchen, looking as pretty and fresh as a flower in a frilly blouse and matching skirt that Paul had sent Teresa to buy when they arrived. Sitting gracefully on a chair, she did not offer to help.

Teresa quickly informed Conchita that she and Luana would be leaving later in the evening. Turning to Luana, she said crisply, "I can handle things here now. You two go and pack your things. There's an old traveling bag in the closet in your room."

As they packed, Luana tried to tell her sister of her fears, but Conchita refused to listen.

"You're always looking for the worst," Conchita said sharply. "If you can't say something cheerful, don't say anything at all!"

Luana bit her lip to keep from spitting out an angry retort. *Perhaps Conchita is right,* she thought, as she quickly folded the few clothes Teresa had purchased and placed them in the old valise. *I always think bad things are coming but that's because it's what I've usually seen. But I don't need to ruin her rosy, hopeful outlook on life.*

The early dinner wasn't a merry meal, in spite of Teresa's and Conchita's efforts to make it so. Paul was moody and remote. Even Conchita's teasing failed to bring a smile to his grim lips. After gulping down a little food, he pushed his chair back almost savagely and went into the living room.

Luana heard him dialing a number on the phone and then his muffled words as he talked. She longed to hear what he was saying, but there was no way she could do so. Obviously he was distressed and angry because once in a while he would raise his voice — and he sounded furious.

Hope began to dawn slightly in Luana's heart. Perhaps these people who were coming to take them away would be those who wouldn't want to murder innocent women!

Paul sent his mother away — to spend the night with a friend — as soon as the dishes were washed and put away. She kissed Luana and Conchita good-bye with tears in her gentle brown eyes. Conchita cried openly, but Luana steeled herself and just wept inside her heart. After all, this was the mother of their enemy!

The dust from the car carrying Teresa away had scarcely settled when a large, shiny Lincoln Continental drove up to the gate. After the driver flashed a card, it was permitted to enter the yard.

As soon as the car drove in, Paul waved Luana and Conchita away from the window where they were watching and took their place. Luana saw him loosen his gun in a shoulder holster that he was wearing openly now. As footsteps sounded on the path, Paul seemed to tense like a rattlesnake ready to strike.

When a ringing knock came at the door, Paul opened it and stood blocking the doorway. "May I see your identification?" he demanded.

Silently he took a card in his hand and studied it. Then he moved back reluctantly, and three men entered the room.

"*Señor* Lawson!" Luana exclaimed in amazement. Relief flowed over her. "Now we have nothing to fear," she told her sister softly. "It is the friend of *Señor* Borders who has been helping to find you."

Lawson's hard eyes softened slightly as they rested on Luana. His keen ears had heard. "*Sí,* you have nothing to fear," he said kindly in Spanish. "We will take you where you will be safe until we need your testimony to put the smugglers forever behind bars where they belong."

"I'm Detective Paul Tanner, sir," Luana was astonished to hear Paul say rather stiffly but respectfully.

Lawson stuck out his hand. "I've heard of you. Understand you're doing a good job. Meet my two lieutenants, Larry Thomas and Bill Jeffreys."

Paul shook hands with Bob Lawson, nodded to his two aides, then said slowly, "I'm amazed, sir, that you would personally take charge of a couple of witnesses."

Luana was glad all the conversation had taken place in Spanish so she and Conchita could understand. Yet she was utterly bewildered by it all.

Lawson laughed easily. "I suppose it does sound rather strange, but I'm not sure you realize how big this case is. These are important witnesses, not only to smuggling aliens across into the United States but also to a drug ring of some magnitude."

"I'm aware of all this, sir. But I just can't understand why you felt it necessary to move the witnesses. Our hiding place is isolated and well guarded by trained and trustworthy officers."

"We're not playing with amateurs out there," Bob said gravely. He leaned slightly toward Paul, "We're talking about a drug bust that will exceed all former busts. And this time we expect to get the drug lord."

His flinty eyes hardened. "This man has surrounded himself with violent men, skilled at murder and any other crimes they feel necessary to remove obstacles to the fulfillment of their greed. So we are taking no chance with these witnesses who may help to convict him."

"I'd like your permission to go with you," Paul said. "I also feel strongly about this case and protecting these girls."

Bob Lawson hesitated and then said amiably, "I see no problem with that. However, you will have to keep in mind that I'm in charge here now. I give the orders!"

"I understand, sir," Paul said.

Luana had tried to follow the conversation closely and now she burst out, "*Señor* Lawson, I do not understand. You mean this-this man — Paul Tanner — is one of your men?"

Lawson chuckled. "Yes, Luana, he's an undercover agent in a narcotics division."

"He's a policeman?" Conchita asked.

"Yes, he's one of our best detectives."

"But-but he was with the *coyotes!*"

"Of course he was," Bob said. "He was gathering information to catch drug dealers. We were sure that some of the smugglers of aliens were also smuggling drugs."

"Then the bottles we carried did contain drugs!"

"We believe so — a fortune in drugs, in fact," Paul suddenly said. "That is why we need you. Your testimonies are part of a plan to put those men in prison."

Conchita moved swiftly to Paul's side and slipped her small hand under his arm. "See, Luana," she said triumphantly. "I knew Paul was not a bad man!"

Luana felt her face grow hot and uncomfortable but she kept her eyes down and said nothing. When she finally did look up, she saw Paul's eyes resting on her with a strange expression on his face.

Then, abruptly, he swung his attention to Bob Lawson. "The girls are packed and ready, sir."

"Good! I would like to use your department's panel truck. It's a government vehicle, is it not? Good! We can carry passengers without anyone seeing who's inside. And our greatest safety for these witnesses may be if we can keep the enemy guessing."

"We'll be taking the guards outside, won't we?" Paul asked.

"No, that's where I draw the line," Lawson said. "My men are absolutely reliable and. . . ."

"I'll vouch for my men."

"No! You can go and no one else. And that's an order," Bob snapped. "Now, let us be on our way immediately."

Within minutes they were on the road.

As they sped through the late afternoon heat, Luana was thankful for the air-conditioning in the vehicle. She could never quite get over the many conveniences these Americans took for granted.

Larry, Lawson's sandy-haired aide was driving, with his superior in front with him. Bill, Paul, Luana, and Conchita sat in the back on comfortable seats attached to each side.

Conchita, after trying unsuccessfully to engage Bill's and Paul's attention across the aisle, slipped to the floor. Curling up like a contented kitten, she was soon fast asleep.

But Luana was uneasy. She didn't know why. Perhaps it was the almost tangible tension Luana sensed in the two men seated across from them.

Bill Jeffreys, Bob Lawson's dark-haired, dark-faced lieutenant was aloof and unfriendly. He ignored the two sisters — and Paul — as if they were not there. Paul had tried a couple of times to make some friendly conversation, but Bill had answered curtly and then lapsed into an alert but remote silence.

The fiery ball was just sinking into the distant horizon, tinting the sky with incredibly beautiful colors when the panel truck finally stopped.

Briskly, the two aides jumped from the truck first, followed by Paul, a yawning Conchita, and Luana. When Luana alighted, she saw that Paul was backed up against the side of the truck.

Bob Lawson and his two lieutenants stood facing him. Directly behind them stood a high rock wall.

Bob Lawson was talking to Paul in English, and Luana felt irritation rise in her. How could she ever understand what was happening?

"I want you to give me your gun now," Lawson said to Paul. "This is my show, and I don't want any interference from you."

"We're back at The Boulders. What's going on?"

"Just bring your gun out very slowly and give it to me." Lawson snapped. "Now!"

Paul's hand was only a blur as a blunt-nosed revolver aimed right at Lawson's heart appeared cradled in his hand. "Don't move a muscle," he ordered Lawson's men, whose hands hovered just over their shoulder holsters, "or your boss is dead!"

"You can't get away with this," Lawson said scornfully. "At one shout my men will come storming from behind that wall and you're coyote meat!"

"But not until you are," Paul said quietly. "Now, I want your two men to give me their guns. You first, Bill, and no tricks. Ease it out and toss it, butt first, over there. Easy now."

Bill hesitated, glancing at Lawson.

"Drop it," Paul thundered menacingly, "or I'll put a bullet right through his heart!"

"Do what he says," Bob said quickly.

Bill, his black eyes smoldering, drew out his gun and tossed it toward Paul's feet.

"Now, it's your turn, Larry," barked Paul.

Luana and Conchita had stood as though turned to stone during the conversation in English. Suddenly, before he could react, Paul saw then felt Luana shove her shoulder hard against him. Completely taken by surprise, he nearly fell. The brief moment was enough. A flash of fire burst from Larry's hand, accompanied by a sharp crack.

Paul's gun fell from nerveless fingers.

Luana and Conchita sprang away, watching with frightened faces.

"Don't shoot him again!" Lawson's sharp order stopped Larry's finger just before it snapped off another shot. "Tanner may have some information that will be beneficial." Bill quickly retrieved his gun and both he and Larry pressed Paul back against the side of the truck, a gun pointed at each side of his head.

Paul's left hand clasped the upper part of his right shoulder, and a red stream ran through his fingers, soaking his right side.

At a quick order from Lawson, Bill turned Paul around roughly and ran his hands over his body. Finding only a knife — which he took — he snapped handcuffs on Paul and slammed him back against the truck.

"Get him inside," Lawson ordered. He pressed a button on a remote control box and the wall slowly slipped apart.

"Paul's hurt, sir," Luana said to Lawson. "What is happening? Is he a *coyote?* His clothes are almost dripping blood. He could bleed to death if his wound isn't cared for."

Bob hesitated and then spoke briskly in Spanish, "She's right, Bill. We don't want this *coyote* to die until he is no longer needed. I saw a first aid kit in the glove compartment. Get it and let the girl patch him up."

Bob tersely ordered Luana and Conchita

to follow him as he walked inside a small courtyard. Then, his men brought Paul and the panel truck inside. The wall slid back into place, looking solid and impenetrable.

"Very ingenious," Paul said sarcastically. His dark eyes were burning as they rested on Bob Lawson. "Am I right in suggesting that you are the king pin that our drug people have been risking our lives the past two years to apprehend?"

Bob threw back his head and laughed. "*Si*, my good man! And I have done everything possible to apprehend him, too!"

Suddenly, a gasp from Conchita distracted both men. "I-it's Pascual and Tiberio. The *coyotes* w-who left you all to die on the desert. What are they doing here?"

The two men, standing partially hidden behind a battered old Volkswagen van, were obviously not anxious to be seen.

"Those two *coyotes* are but little two-bit peons in the service of the chief smuggler," Paul said harshly in Spanish. "None other than your protector, Bob Lawson."

Luana whipped around. "That cannot be so! He is our friend — and the friend of Richard Borders who was so kind to us."

"Ask him yourself!" Paul said brutally.

Luana turned toward Bob Lawson and suddenly didn't need his answer.

The eyes watching hers were cruel, derisive — and triumphant. "Thank you for your help, *Señorita* Torres," he said with a mocking little bow.

Luana turned in anguish to Paul and whispered, "What have I done?"

Paul, his jaw set in stern lines, stared at her bleakly until she dropped her eyes.

Luana turned back to Lawson and spoke falteringly, "How could you do this to me when I-I trusted you?"

Bob's thin smile was frosty. "*That* has been your problem all along. You are too trusting. First you trusted *coyotes* who left you to die and then you trusted everyone at The Boulders just because they were kind to you. The lesson you have learned too late is: never trust anyone."

"No! It cannot be! I just trusted the wrong ones," Luana whispered, despair plain in her voice. She glanced again at Paul but then quickly away again. "What a fool I have been!" Anguish, shame, and fear clawed across her face.

Paul, Luana, and Conchita were pushed into a small room. As soon as Bill unlocked Paul's handcuffs, he sat down on a rough chair and gripped his shoulder.

Tossing a small first aid kit on the floor, Lawson ordered Luana. "Bind up Detective

Tanner's wound. I don't want him to bleed all over the floor."

Swiftly Luana went to Paul and knelt before him. "Let me see," she said gently. Beads of sweat stood out on his strong forehead and ran down into his eyes.

Wincing slightly, he peeled off his blood-soaked shirt. He saw her sway when she saw the hole from which blood bubbled.

"Take a big wad of cotton and wrap some bandages around it and hold it right here," Paul directed through clenched teeth. "No, harder than that. There, that should stop the bleeding soon. Just keep pressure there until the blood clots."

Conchita had come to stand nearby. She laid her shapely hand on Paul's forehead and soothed back the damp black hair.

"Are you happy, Luana?" she said sarcastically. "You helped that wicked man shoot Paul and capture us. I hope you feel proud!"

Tears blurred Luana's eyes as she turned her head away so Paul could not see her cry. When she spoke, it was in a stricken voice. "You are right, Conchita. I'm completely to blame! If I had not shoved Paul, there is a good chance we could all have escaped.

"B-but, Paul, I-I couldn't understand the English you were speaking, and I-I thought you were going to harm us — not help us.

I-I'm so sorry," she quavered. "I did not know *Señor* Lawson and his men were the real *coyotes*. P-please forgive me?"

"It's a little late for that, don't you think?" Paul replied bitterly.

20

Terry was in a black mood. In the three days since he and his family had left The Boulders, they had been sightseeing in the Tucson area, visited Saguaro National Monument, Old Tucson, and other sights. This noon, after visiting the Arizona–Sonora Desert Museum, they had picnicked in the Tucson Mountain Park adjoining it.

Determined to forget Nica and her hallucinations, he had told himself that she was out of his life — and good riddance — but her strange story haunted him.

But, he rationalized, *I promised to not tell anyone.*

He was angry — at Nica, at himself, at everyone — as he climbed down into a dry creek bed that wound around the picnic site. The tall brush and small desert trees that crowded close to the banks of the arroyo forced Terry to look up. The rock-walled, covered picnic shelter where his folks were was barely visible.

"Terry," Joy called, "don't go far. You could get lost."

"I won't," he called back.

"We'll be leaving in about twenty minutes," his father added.

"Okay, I'll be back in time," he answered. He was relieved they hadn't made him go back. A few minutes alone might help him sort out his feelings.

He came to a "Y" in the creek bed. He looked longingly toward the fork that led off to the west and disappeared around a hill but decided he had better take the fork that wound around the campground. He didn't have time for the longer one.

Perspiration stung his sunburned face as he tramped along the pebbly creek bottom. "Arizona is the hottest place I ever saw," he muttered in irritation. Taking off his cap, he fanned his hot face. The breeze touched his sweat-soaked hair bringing a brief, welcome coolness to his head.

He sighed. Why did life have to be so complicated, anyway? Ever since Nica had given him her graphic account of a helpless little white dog being sacrificed by a satanic priest, and the biggest lie yet — that she had almost been sacrificed when she was a tiny child — Terry had been wrestling with the feeling that he should tell his parents. He knew the fantastic story wasn't true, but maybe Nica needed psychiatric help.

He hadn't felt particularly badly at telling about seeing Paul Tanner on the rooftop at The Boulders even when he had promised him he wouldn't. But Paul was committing a serious crime and that was different than this.

Or was it? Nica was using drugs and that was illegal, too. She needed help. "But she would hate me forever if I told on her," he said aloud.

A slight sound behind him startled him. He started to turn around when a powerful, tobacco-scented hand clamped over his mouth and strong fingers pinned his arms to his sides.

Terry struggled wildly but knew he was helpless in the steel-like hands of his captor.

A second man, a lean, long-haired Mexican, moved out in front of Terry. "You weel come with us." The man's voice held soft menace as he reached out and gripped Terry's arm until he winced.

Terry struggled, trying to bite the hand that covered his mouth.

"Do that again and you weel get a broken jaw!" his captor growled in an accented voice.

Almost lifting his slight figure from the

ground, the men started to climb up the creek bank.

Suddenly, Terry heard Joy calling him. He intensified his struggles, trying to tear the man's hand from across his mouth. He could hear the crunch of Joy's footsteps on the gravel of the creek bed.

The men half turned, and Terry saw Joy round a little bend and stop suddenly as she saw the two men holding Terry. Then she rushed forward. "Stop!" she screamed. "That's my son! Take your hands off him!"

One of the men swore savagely. The lean Mexican drew out a wicked looking knife and laid it across Terry's throat. "If you yell again or make any noise, I weel use this on the *muchacho*," he threatened. Joy stopped just a few yards from the men, her blue eyes wide with fright.

"D-don't hurt him," she quavered. "What do you want?"

"Come over here, and don't make a sound," the man motioned with the knife.

Joy moved slowly forward and stopped a couple of feet from the men. "I-if you want money, I'll get it for you. But don't hurt us."

"Don't talk! Just do what I say and you weel not be hurt. *Sabe?*"

Her glance at Terry was filled with terror,

but his stepmother nodded her head that she understood.

Without removing his hand from Terry's mouth, the shorter, stocky Mexican swung Terry around until his other arm was wrapped about Terry's thin chest, with his arms pinned down.

"Be still or I weel crush you like a bug!" his captor growled, when Terry tried to struggle against the bone-crunching hold. He squeezed and Terry gasped against the pain and pressure. The sky seemed to darken and there was a loud hum in his head. Then his captor relaxed his grip enough for Terry to breathe again.

"Let's get out of here, Tiberio."

"*Si*, Pascual. If you two make a sound, we weel slice you to peeces and feed you to the buzzards!" Terry's captor threatened. "Do you understand? Both of you!"

Terry saw Joy nod fearfully. When Terry didn't respond, his captor tightened his arm around his chest. Terry nodded agreement instantly. His chest throbbed with pain when the man loosened his hold. He wondered hazily if his ribs were broken.

Pascual clambered up the narrow bank, half-dragging Joy with him, and peered out into the picnic park. Terry wished fervently that they had not chosen this rugged picnic ground. Each site provided a measure of privacy for picnickers. And privacy was not what they needed right now!

"All ees clear," Pascual said, as he pulled Joy swiftly onto the rim of the embankment that was screened by brush from the campground clearing. Tiberio followed him and in a few quick steps, they were at the side of an old Volkswagen van, parked at a bend of the little ravine.

The kidnappers dumped them roughly on the floor. Dirty rags were tied to their mouths, and their hands and feet were bound tightly with rope. The stocky Mexican, Tiberio, slid behind the wheel and the old Volkswagen crept out of the park and onto the paved road where it picked up speed and was soon racing through the hot afternoon.

Gingerly, Terry rolled from side to side. His chest still felt raw and bruised but, with extreme relief, he decided no ribs were broken.

After a few minutes, Pascual said something in Spanish. At Tiberio's muffled answer, Pascual jumped in back and squatted down between them on the floor.

He pulled out the thin, long knife and sliced it suggestively in the air. "I am going to be nice to you two. It ees hot so I weel take off the rags from your mouths. But if you yell for help I weel —" He swished the knife in the air not far from Joy's pale face.

At Terry's frightened gasp, he grinned, showing yellow teeth. When the rags were removed, they drew in deep gulps of air gratefully. Joy thanked her captor with a faint voice. Looking pleased with himself, the young Mexican climbed back into the front seat.

After a few minutes Terry rolled to his side and whispered to Joy, "A-are they going to k-kill us?"

"Let's pray together right now," Joy said softly. "God knows where we are and He will take care of us."

The old van rattled through the desert under a blistering sun. A distant roll of thunder and black clouds forming on the horizon went unheeded. As Joy prayed, Terry felt his heart seem to swell, and then tears rolled down his cheeks.

21

"What are these men going to do to us?" Terry asked, as Joy finished praying.

"I don't know," Joy acknowledged. "But let's try to be as calm and cooperative as we can. We've got to trust that God is working."

But even as she tried to soothe Terry, Joy felt a big knot of fear in her own throat. What did these men want with them? Were they after ransom? *Dear God,* she prayed silently, *you're our only hope of rescue. Be with Skye — and us.*

The heat was oppressive but before long, she heard a soft snore and realized Terry had fallen asleep. Rolling about to make herself more comfortable, she tried to relax, too. She wanted to be ready for whatever lay ahead.

Some time later she awoke with a start. The van was no longer moving! The side doors of the vehicle opened and rough brown hands pulled them out.

Joy squinted against the blinding brightness of the sun. Leaning against the van, she tried to balance herself on bound feet. Tiberio pushed her to a sitting position and untied her hands and feet, then Terry's. They were inside a small courtyard, formed partially by high walls and partly by what appeared to be storage rooms.

As they were shoved toward one of the nearest doors, Terry leaned over and whispered, "We're back at The Boulders."

Joy gasped and forgot to move forward in her astonishment. Tiberio irritably shoved her toward the door. Pascual took out a key, opened the door, and pushed the two inside a large dim room.

"The Boulders?" Joy said incredulously as soon as they were inside. When Terry insisted they were, Joy asked how he knew.

"This is where I saw the two men unloading Luana's sister from that same old Volkswagen van," Terry said adamantly. "I was on the roof above this courtyard."

Suddenly, Terry snapped his fingers and exclaimed, "I thought I had seen Pascual before! He was one of the two men!"

"B-but how could we be at The Boulders? And . . ." A new thought struck Joy. "Luana said the two smugglers who left them to die in the desert — and took Conchita away — were named Pascual and Tiberio!" She drew in her breath sharply. "Terry, these men are murderers!"

"It sure looks like that's who they are."

"But what are they doing at The Boulders?"

Terry's eyes met Joy's dazed stare. "We all thought Paul Tanner was in a smuggling ring with Pascual and the others. Yet Paul was the one who kidnapped Conchita from Pascual."

"This is a confusing mess," Joy said. "Is Mr. Borders a smuggler, too? Wouldn't he have to know if the *coyotes* bring prisoners here?"

"The house is huge and rambles all over inside the hill," Terry said slowly. "He may know, of course, but I think we are in a place that has a hidden door to it. I'm almost sure that the courtyard Mr. Borders showed me — and later Bill Jeffreys showed me — is not this one, the one Paul kidnapped the girl from."

Terry pulled out his wallet and took a small red thread from it, handing it to Joy. "I found a hall that should have had a door leading out to the roof, and there was no longer a door there. I don't think I was confused. I think there had been a door, but it had been hidden some way. This thread was caught between two bricks, and it took some force to pull it out. See, it's red as blood."

Joy held the thread under the window by the door. Then, she heard Terry whisper in a strangled voice, "It's the Satan worship place."

Shocked, Joy turned to look into the dimness of the room. The large room they stood in was draped in black, its floor covered with a scarlet rug. Near the far end stood a long, coffin-like altar, lined with a skull, black candles, and goblets. Behind the pulpit hung a black banner strewn with blood-red pentagrams.

Chills trickled over Joy's body. "What do you mean, the Satan worship room?" Joy asked. She felt as if her heart was trying to pound its way out of her body.

"Nica showed it to me, only it was in a different place then. Nica told me they had moved it. First to the pool area and then here, I guess."

"What is going on?" Joy asked. "Why didn't you tell your father and me that there was a room like this at The Boulders?"

"I promised Nica I wouldn't," Terry answered. He started walking down the length of the room. Joy followed. At the end of the long altar, Terry let his eyes travel down its length and then back. Suddenly, he bent over and studied a dark stain.

"There're the stains Nica said she

thought were blood," he said softly, as if he had forgotten Joy's presence. "Yes, this is the same altar that was in the room in the storage area of the house."

An icy trail of fear ran down Joy's backbone, and she shivered. What dreadful evil was reaching its horrible fingers toward her, her family, and her friends?

22

Luana had found a water faucet in the tiny, dirty bathroom in a corner of the room where they were imprisoned and cleansed Paul's wound with bandage and cotton from the first aid kit. In spite of her carefulness, it began to bleed again, and she had to hold a bandage over it until the flow ceased. Then she doused his wound with Merthiolate, causing Paul to wince.

"At least the blood should have washed the wound clean," Paul said matter-of-factly.

"But the bullet is still in there so that is not good," Luana said worriedly.

"I don't think the bullet broke a bone, though. So I'm lucky — or Mama's prayers helped."

Luana looked at his face quickly. He was looking very serious and sober, as if such a possibility had just occurred to him.

"You are going to be all right," Conchita said, her soft voice husky with feeling. She rested a soft palm possessively on his shoulder. "But I know it must hurt terribly."

Irritation with Conchita washed over Luana. Why must Conchita feel it forever necessary to flirt with every male around! Strangely Conchita's coquetry had never bothered her so much before.

Glancing up, she saw Paul's amused eyes upon her and felt her face grow hot. She had never been adept at concealing her feelings, and the man must have read her face like a book! She dropped her eyes in embarrassment and confusion.

"Ouch!"

In her haste to cover her confusion, Luana had reached for a fresh bandage and bumped Paul's wounded shoulder. "I-I'm sorry," she said miserably.

She finished bandaging his shoulder as rapidly as possible, then walked over to a small, dirty window that looked out on the courtyard. She felt extremely sorry for herself. Poor as dirt, plain and skinny, too. And as clumsy as they come! Why was life so unfair?

She leaned her head on the stone frame and sighed. They had started for this magical place called the United States so full of dreams and hopes. Now it seemed as if death was to be their only freedom.

"Don't give up hope," Paul's voice said gently at her shoulder.

She felt a rush of tears and turned her face away in shame. Angry at herself for letting Paul see her cry, she brushed her eyes on her sleeve and tried to laugh. "I-I'm sorry. I don't usually c-cry like this."

"I know, you've always had to be strong," Paul said softly.

Again, tears stung her eyes. She *had* always been the one who comforted, not the one who was comforted. She didn't know how to cope with sympathy.

Paul turned to stare out the window, choosing to ignore her teary eyes, to Luana's intense relief. "Tell me about your life in Mexico," he said. When she was silent, he asked, "Was it so terrible there that you would risk your life to enter this country illegally?"

"It was unbearable!" Conchita said, coming up behind them. "Work! Work! Work! And all it got us was barely enough food to keep us alive. How lucky you are to live in *Norte America!*" She sighed wistfully and her lovely lips drooped. "If I have to go back to Mexico, I think I will die!"

"You will probably get your wish — to die I mean!" Luana said sarcastically.

Ignoring Luana, Conchita said softly to Paul, "You really should lie down. You have lost much blood and that surely has made you weak. Come." She tucked her shapely hand under his elbow and tugged. "Let me help you over to that cot."

"My shoulder hurts like crazy and I'm a little weak, but I'm certainly not helpless," Paul said with a crooked grin. But he yielded to Conchita's coaxing and allowed her to lead him to a cot in the corner. He stretched out with a grateful sigh, and Conchita made much of fluffing up the hard pillow and tucking it under his head.

She found a reasonably clean piece of rag, wet it, and began to smooth it gently over his temples and forehead.

"Thanks," Paul murmured, "that does feel good." Within a minute he was breathing deeply, evenly.

Luana tried to ignore them. What did she care if Conchita made Paul love her! They were all going to die anyway, so Conchita was wasting her efforts! But in spite of her gallant protestations, Luana's heart ached with bitterness.

Staring stoically out the window, Luana admitted the truth to herself. She had always lived in Conchita's shadow. Although eight years older than Conchita, her sister was the one who had matured to become lovely in face and form — much too young. She, the older daughter, had almost starved herself to insure that her little sister, and their sickly mother had enough food.

Luana's naturally thin face had matured into a plainness that hurt her to look at in the mirror, and her body had grown tough and strong but had remained skinny and boyish. No young man had ever looked at her twice. Especially since there was always Conchita to catch their eye!

Conchita teased and flirted but adamantly refused marriage with any of her many suitors. When Luana remonstrated with her for "leading young men on," Conchita would toss her long dark hair impishly and say that she must have some entertainment.

"But I will never — no, never! — marry anyone except someone who can get me a green card so I can live in the United States!"

Footsteps at the door broke Luana's reverie; then came a rattle of keys, and Pascual stood in the doorway. "You girls come with me. It's supper time and there's no reason we men should fix food when there are women around to do it for us."

He smirked in the direction of Conchita. "Besides, some girls are more fun to look at than a man."

Conchita flounced up and came to stand by Luana. "Why should we fix a meal for you? You left my sister and the others to die in the desert."

"Jose did that," Pascual protested. "He swore he was going back and take water to the *pollos*."

"Well, you took me with you, drugged me, and then left me to die like the other illegals! *Señor* Borders' men said they found me wandering in the desert."

"Ah, that just isn't so," Pascual said coaxingly. "I would never leave a pretty thing like you in the desert."

"Let's stop all the foolishness and fix a meal for these jackals," Luana broke in ungraciously. She moved past Pascual into the courtyard.

He led the way to a room across the courtyard. Inside was an electric hotplate, a table, and a small cabinet containing a few dishes, cutlery, and a few pots and pans. A large ice chest sat on the floor.

"There're cans of stuff in that sack," Pascual said, pointing to a large paper bag on the table.

Luana quickly took stock of the supplies, and within a short while she and her sister had a large pan of rolled enchiladas setting on the table, complete with red and green salsa. Fresh coffee perked in a pot on the stove.

Three Mexican men besides Pascual and Tiberio came at Conchita's call — leering at Conchita as they filled enamel plates and went back outside to lean against the wall to eat in the shade of a building. The men ate leisurely, with much joking and laughing.

When the men had finished eating, Tiberio ordered the girls to prepare two more plates of food. Luana went to the window and watched him carry the two plates into a room not far from their own cell.

"There are two other prisoners here," she informed Conchita. "I wish I could have seen who they are."

"I saw a face at that window when we came," Conchita said. "It appeared to be a blond-headed boy."

"Kidnapping children, too!" Luana said in disgust.

"I'm going to fix Paul something to eat," Conchita said, piling a plate high.

"If he eats all of that, he's a mighty hungry man," Luana said caustically.

Conchita turned around and looked at Luana. Then placing one shapely hand on her hip, she smiled sweetly, "You're jealous because Paul likes me. You want him to like you."

Luana sniffed, but felt hot blood stain her face as she turned away without speaking.

Conchita called to Pascual that she had a plate ready for Paul and could she take it over. But he took it from her, ordered them to eat, and then to clean up the dishes.

"Whatever you say," Conchita said sweetly. But when he left to deliver the food to Paul, Luana heard her say under her breath, "You stinking old lizard!"

When they had finished cleaning up and were led back to their cell, Luana saw that Paul was sitting up on the cot. Only a small portion of food was missing from the plate. Before she could say anything, Conchita rushed over, sat down beside Paul and gushed, "You didn't eat hardly anything. Are you feeling worse?"

"I'm okay," Paul said tersely. "Just my shoulder aches."

He looked at Luana standing by the door, "I'm just racking my mind trying to think of a way out of here. Have you any ideas?"

"I wish I did," Luana said.

"If we only had a weapon of some kind," Paul said. "They searched me and took my knife, as well as my gun. Have either of you girls seen anything around here that could be used for a weapon?"

"Would this help?" Luana asked. Turning

around, she reached inside the neck of her dress. When she turned back to Paul a slim knife lay in her hand.

"Great!" Paul said. "Let me have it." His approving words caused a shaft of joy to quiver through her.

"I found it in the back of the cabinet drawer so maybe it won't be missed," Luana said.

Paul stood up to walk over to her and swayed. Instantly, Luana was at his side.

"You're hot, feverish. I'll get you some aspirin from the first aid kit, then you really should lie down and rest."

Paul tried to protest that he was all right, but Luana was adamant. "You must get your strength back in case you get a chance to use this. I'll get you some water."

"Okay," he agreed reluctantly. Swallowing the aspirin with the tepid water, he lay back down. Within minutes, he was sound asleep.

Luana watched him uneasily. *He falls asleep too quickly,* she thought. *I hope his shoulder isn't getting infected.*

Conchita came over and whispered rather crossly that she, too, was tired. "I'm taking a nap now, too," she said a little sulkily as she lay down on the other cot.

Luana secreted the knife under the foot of

Paul's mattress, then sat down in one of the two chairs, tipping it back against the wall. It wasn't as comfortable as a cot, but it wasn't too bad.

She dozed off and was startled awake by a scuffing sound. Snapping upright, she let the chair fall with a jarring click. Paul was standing near her.

"Where is the knife?" he whispered.

She got it for him. After testing its sharpness, and proclaiming it not bad, he slipped it back under the mattress.

"I feel like talking," Paul said softly. "Come over here and sit with me on the cot."

Luana complied, sitting on the far end. Now that she was no longer angry with Paul, she was very much aware of him as a ruggedly good-looking man. His proximity caused her heart to do crazy things.

Paul's eyes crinkled with amusement. "I promise not to bite you."

Luana edged a little closer to him.

"Now, I asked you a while ago why you crossed over into our country. Tell me about it."

Paul's dark eyes were kind, so Luana began self-consciously to tell of her life in Mexico. Before long, she found she could talk freely and comfortably with this man.

"I've had a very dull life, I'm afraid," she said. "My mother was never very strong, and when I was only six-years-old, my father died. I don't remember him. But both he and my mother were from extremely poor families."

Luana's voice softened. "Mother was very pretty — like Conchita — and it wasn't long until she was married again to a dashing young man — handsome and carefree — but as selfish as they come: Alfonso Torres."

"Conchita's father?"

"*Si*. He was gone much of the time after he grew tired of mother — which was within a few weeks. She idolized him, though, and made excuses for him; never saying a critical word about him or allowing anyone else to. I grew to despise him as I saw Mother grow old before her time — killing herself — trying to keep bread on our table and rags on our backs."

"So you tried to take as much off of her as you could," Paul said gently.

Luana looked at him. "Yes. I was the oldest and it was my place. Before I was nine I was doing all the housework, cooking, and washing, so Mother could wash and iron and sew other people's clothes for a few *pesos*."

Luana's voice trembled with suppressed

rage. "Now and then Alfonso would come home, well-dressed and well-fed, and boss us all around like a lord and then leave again after a few days. He ate up what little food we had and took away any money Mother had managed to make. Mother would be so happy for those few days and the few crumbs of affection that-that despicable man threw her!"

"He never helped support you at all?" Paul asked.

"Never! He seemed to think we should be honored to have his presence whenever he chose to come back," Luana stopped for a moment and took a deep breath to calm her agitation. "When I was twelve, he came home for the last time. We heard later that he was killed by a jealous husband in a bar in the United States." Tears suddenly filled Luana's eyes, but she was unaware of them as she looked full in Paul's face. "But it didn't happen soon enough. One of the times he came home he had brought mother a disease — a venereal disease. She was already sick when he came the last time, but she didn't know what was wrong with her. Since Mother was not strong anyway, mercifully, she didn't live to suffer very long."

"Then you took care of Conchita?"

"Yes, we had few relatives, and they had

families of their own and were very poor. Even before Mother died Conchita and I were talking of trying to come to America. Conchita's father always talked about the United States as if it were the promised land."

"You despised Alfonso and yet you bear his last name?"

"Alfonso insisted I use Torres, his name," Luana said. "I don't even recall my own father's name." For a moment she was silent, then she said suddenly, "You remind me much of Alfonso. Not that I think you are like him." She hastened to add, "You are not as handsome for one thing. . . ."

Luana dropped her eyes in embarrassment. "That is a terrible thing to say to a man," she said miserably. "I'm sorry. It isn't that you are not nice-looking but. . . ." Her face flamed red and she muttered, "I always say the wrong thing!"

Paul was laughing. "Well, at least I know what you think of my looks. I like your honesty."

"Please don't laugh at me," Luana said tragically. "I didn't mean to-to run down your looks. All the handsome young men I have ever known were selfish, conceited, and mean. I could never trust a really handsome man," she said earnestly.

Paul was no longer laughing, or even smiling. He reached over and took one of Luana's slim hands in a strong brown hand and said softly, "You are a breath of fresh air, a priceless pearl. Honesty is something seldom seen in a girl these days. I like you!"

Luana was struck absolutely dumb. Was this a new line? She had heard many young men talking to Conchita and what she didn't hear, Conchita had always filled her in on. But Paul was not like any of those young men. Perhaps American men were different from Mexican young men.

Finally, she found her tongue. Drawing her hand away she said quickly, "I have told you about myself, but I know nothing about you, except that your mother is Teresa."

"Yes, Teresa is my mother — and she is a wonderful woman. Perhaps she is why I never married. No girl I ever knew could compare with her." He hesitated, then added, "Strangely, her life was similar in some ways to your mother. She met and married the wrong man."

"A white man?" Luana asked. "If Tanner is your real name."

"Yes, my father was a *gringo* — David Tanner. While he was in his last year of college, my father became very sick and his parents sent him to a clinic in Mexico.

"My mother's father and grandfather owned and operated a clothing store and had a nice home. David Tanner came to live in their home while he was recovering from his illness."

"And she fell in love with the handsome *gringo?*"

"Yes, and when my father found out my mother was to bear his child, he did the right thing and married her. I believe he really loved her — at least my mother thought so."

Paul's face grew stony. "But when his wealthy family heard that their son — the only son and heir to the family name and wealth had married a Mexican girl, they were horrified. They refused to acknowledge the marriage and demanded that he divorce her."

"And he did?"

"Not at first. He begged his parents to at least meet his wife. They refused. For a few months the phone lines and the mail service grew red hot with correspondence. Finally, they persuaded my father to come home for a conference. He never returned!"

"I'm so sorry," Luana said.

"Mother cried for weeks, my aunt told me. She wouldn't eat and she couldn't sleep. Finally her father became very angry and told her she had a child to think of — his grandchild! So she came back to the land of the living for my sake!"

"How do you happen to live in the United States?"

"My father's lawyers set up a trust fund that took care of my mother and me and also paid for my education. And she was given the choice of coming to the States before the divorce, if she would not try to contact my father in any way."

"So she came to the United States before you were born?"

"Right! I think Mother lived in hopes for a long time that her David would come to her, but he never did. With money from my father's family, she bought a small house, learned perfect English, and waited for her husband to come back to her."

"How sad," Luana said.

"Yes, I hated him for a long time, but she finally got it through my thick skull that at least his family was honorable enough to provide for us. There would have been nothing we could have done if he had left us dependent upon her family in Mexico.

"So now I feel grateful, though I could never love a man who would desert his wife."

"You have never met him?"

"I have no desire to."

"Why did you decide to be a detective and fight drugs?"

Paul's laugh was edged in bitterness. "Not for a very noble reason, I guess. My Latin blood caused me a lot of hassles. I got it from both Hispanics and whites — I was a half-breed. I decided to become a cop because people looked up to them.

"While I was a rookie cop, I saw the horrors of drugs first hand. Sometimes I could hardly sleep; for days, I just couldn't forget. That's when I made the decision to go undercover and fight to keep drugs out of our country! I hate drugs and drug-traffickers with a passion," Paul said harshly.

"Do you have a girlfriend?" Luana blurted out and then could have bitten her tongue off in horror at her boldness. What had made her ask such a thing? Suddenly she realized the question had hovered in the back of her mind ever since she had found out Paul was not a *coyote*.

Paul looked at her sharply, then laughed shortly. "No, I don't have a girl, and I don't need one! In this business I never know if I'll live through the night!"

He glanced over at Conchita, looking lovely even while deep in sleep. "But I did have a girl once. Just like your sister — almost too beautiful to be true — except her long hair was blonde and her eyes were green. She was an illegal alien from Honduras.

"I couldn't believe such an angel of a girl would fall in love with me. But she declared her undying love, and fool that I was, I asked her to marry me!"

His voice grew harsh, "Fortunately, I accidentally found out before we were married that she didn't love me at all. She just wanted my name so she could get a green card to live in the United States! I'd never marry an illegal alien if I wanted to marry — which I don't!"

"Well, don't think I was interested in marrying you!" Luana sputtered angrily. "I don't know what possessed me to ask you such a question anyway!"

Paul grinned suddenly. "Did you know that your eyes seem to shoot sparks when you're angry? Then you're almost pretty."

"You don't have to make fun of me," she said tartly. "I know I'm not pretty like Conchita, but you didn't have to say so!"

"You told me I wasn't handsome so we're even now," Paul said with a wicked glint in his eyes.

"I didn't say you weren't handsome, I. . . ." Luana floundered to a stop, knowing her face was flaming and hearing Paul's delighted chuckle.

Overcome with embarrassment, Luana dropped her eyes and said the first thing that came to her mind. "Your mother never married again?"

"No, she is a one-man woman, it seems. She has had opportunity, but she has devoted herself to me — and to her church."

Luana's voice was sad. "My mother was devoted to her church, too, but it never seemed to give her real peace. I wish now she had known that Jesus could bring peace and joy — like *Señora* Windthorn talked about."

"That must be the kind of church my mother attends," Paul said soberly. "It is not the kind she grew up in. But a lady befriended us soon after we moved here, and after a while, Mother began to go to church with her. Her God seems to give her much happiness. I have often wished I had what she has."

"Why don't you?"

"I guess I always felt God would object to what I want to do with my life."

"Have you ever thought that perhaps you are right where He wants you, fighting for what's good and right?" Luana asked thoughtfully.

Paul looked startled. "Could that be?" His eyes narrowed. "Are you a Christian like my mother?"

"No," Luana said wistfully, "but I think I would like to be. *Señora* Windthorn told me of the peace God has given to her and her husband and the wonderful things He did for them. I think I, too, would like to serve God."

"We could use a little help from God right now," Paul said grimly.

Luana looked at him quickly.

The sound of footsteps on the pavement outside interrupted them. The key rattled in the lock and Bob Lawson walked in, flanked by his two lieutenants. As Luana saw his icy, greenish eyes sweep over her and rest on Paul, fear constricted her throat.

Those eyes blazed with a cruel, wolfish gleam.

23

The message was waiting for Skye at their hotel, printed in pencil on a child's writing tablet. The poorly-formed letters of the note were barely readable.

When Joy and Terry had vanished without a trace, Skye had presumed that they had taken a wrong turn and couldn't find their way back to the picnic site quickly. He berated himself that he had allowed Joy to go after Terry, but he had not been greatly alarmed.

When the two did not return after a short while, Skye and Mitzie had begun to call. Then he had taken Mitzie with him, and they had gone completely around the campground, following the arroya Terry had taken, calling every few yards.

After that they had remembered the other fork of the gully and had followed it quite a while with no results. Thoroughly alarmed by this time, Skye had found the park rangers. When they had turned up no sign of his wife and son, the sheriff's department had been called immediately. To be lost on the desert even for a day could be disastrous in the summer.

After hours of fruitless searching, Sheriff Gomez had suggested he call the hotel, in case a message had been left for him.

Skye had called and when he was informed there was a letter for him in the lobby, he asked the desk attendant to open it and read it over the telephone.

"It's pretty hard to read, like the one who wrote it could barely print," the desk clerk said apologetically after he opened it.

Skye's face went as white as ashes, as he listened to the note:

"We hav yer wife an boy. We call later to tell whur mony be left to pay fer them."

"Has somebody kidnapped Mother and Terry?" Mitzie asked in a terrified whisper.

Skye put his arm around his small daughter and said quickly, "Yes, but we'll find them." He wished he felt as confident as his words.

The sheriff reached for the phone. "Let me talk to the desk clerk."

Silently, numb with shock, Skye handed him the telephone. Mitzie clutched his hand and began to sob convulsively. "W-what if we n-never see them a-again?"

He wrapped her in his arms and held her,

saying all the soothing things he could think of while a knife slowly turned, cutting his heart to ribbons. The same horrible fear was trying to eat itself into his own heart like an ugly leech!

Skye forced his mind to listen to the words of Sheriff Gomez asking the clerk questions about who had brought the message, what time had it come, and if he had seen anyone suspicious hanging around the lobby earlier.

Mitzie drew away from Skye and said in a trembling voice, "W-who kidnapped them?"

"We don't know yet, but we will get them back, Mitzie. You've got to believe that!"

"What d-do the kidnappers want?"

"The note said we would be told how much money to give them," Skye said. "And we'll do whatever we have to do to get them back," he assured her.

The sheriff hung up the phone. "Did you find out anything helpful?" Skye asked.

"Not really," the sheriff replied. "But at least we know they aren't wandering around out in the desert. The clerk didn't know who brought the letter or when it came. We'll talk to him some more, however, and also to the other employees.

"Now, I would suggest you and your daughter go back to your hotel and wait by the phone until you hear from the kidnappers again. We want you to work closely with us on this so we not only get your people back but the kidnappers, too."

Mitzie began to sob again. "D-daddy, wh-what if we n-never find M-Mother and Terry? How could we ever b-bear it?"

"Mitzie!" Skye spoke firmly, though gently. "Don't even think it! God is still God! Let's just believe that He is going to bring them back. We'll pray right now and tell Him about our fears and pain." The spoken words sheared away the doubts from his own heart and replaced them with hope.

The sheriff looked a little startled when Skye took his daughter's hands in his and prayed as earnestly as if he were in church, instead of on the street in front of a phone booth.

"Heavenly Father, you know where Joy and Terry are. We ask that you protect them and bring them back to us safely. Give us and the sheriff's department guidance in our search. Please give us all strength through this ordeal. We're scared, Lord, but we trust you. And we thank you humbly."

24

"There's someone else here!" Terry said excitedly.

Joy jumped up and moved quickly to the small dusty window where Terry stood and looked out. Two girls disappeared into a doorway. "I wonder who they could be?"

"There's a big, dark blue van in the courtyard. I didn't even hear it come in."

"Probably came while we were searching the room trying to find a way out," Joy said.

Suddenly a key turned in the lock and a tall, thin man entered the room.

"Mr. Lawson!" Joy exclaimed in extreme relief. "Are we ever glad to see you! Two horrible men kidnapped us and put us in this awful room."

Bob Lawson's piercing eyes softened and his thin lips curved into a little smile. "Don't worry about a thing, Mrs. Windthorn. I'll get you out of here real soon. But first I need to ask some questions."

"Did you have us brought here?" Terry

asked, suddenly. His eyes narrowed doubtfully. "You-you aren't one of the smugglers, are you?"

"Don't be ridiculous!" Lawson said sharply. "Let's sit down and talk for a bit," Lawson said more kindly, leading them away from the window to the side of the room. Pulling three chairs up, he set two side by side and motioned Joy and Terry into them. He took the other facing them.

"Now," he said firmly to Terry, "I need to know what Richard's daughter, Nica, told you the other day when you were at the pool together."

"She-she told me not to tell what she said," Terry said hesitantly.

"But you told your parents, didn't you?" Lawson prodded.

"No! I didn't tell anyone what she said. I promised I wouldn't."

"Tell us what?" Joy asked, puzzled.

Lawson ignored Joy. "You didn't tell your parents? Do you think that was wise, not telling them Nica was using drugs and telling weird stories?"

Joy gasped. "Nica uses drugs?"

"I guess it wasn't very smart not to tell," Terry mumbled, dropping his eyes from Lawson's piercing gaze and Joy's astonished one. "I-I've been worried about not telling because Nica could become a drug addict but-but I hated to break my promise."

"You didn't tell your sister or anyone else? Look at me, Terry. Is that right?" Bob asked.

"That's right," Terry agreed, meeting Bob's eyes reluctantly.

"Did Nica tell where she got the drugs?" Lawson's gimlet eyes seemed to bore into Terry's.

"Yes, she found them in a little bottle in the Satan worship place."

Lawson expressed no surprise when Terry mentioned a Satan worship room, Joy noticed. He must know *about it!* She thought. *I wonder if Nica's father knows? Or did he set it up?* Worried and frightened now, she gripped Terry's hand as Lawson went on with his questioning.

"Did Nica say how the drugs came to be in that room?"

"Why — no. I guess whoever set up the room put them there."

"How did you find that room?"

"Nica was exploring the house and found it," Joy interjected. "She took Terry to see it. He told me."

"And what did you and Skye think when you found out there was a place for satanic worship in Richard Borders' house?" Lawson asked Joy.

216

"We didn't know about it. Terry told me after we were brought here. What is going on anyway? The two smugglers who left the illegals to die in the desert are around here. Have you arrested them?"

"Why didn't you tell your parents about the room?" Bob asked Terry, ignoring Joy's question.

"It-it was Nica's secret," Terry explained. "She would have been mad if I had told." Terry dropped his head and muttered, "I-I guess I should have told."

"So your parents knew absolutely nothing about the satanic room or that Nica was using drugs?"

"No, we didn't," Joy said, beginning to be impatient. "Why are you asking all of these questions? Has something happened to Nica?"

Lawson said gravely, "Not yet, but I'm concerned for her. Nica *is* using drugs. She could get in serious trouble. Terry, I want you to tell me every detail of how Nica found the drugs and what she said about everything. It could be important."

"Do you think someone at The Boulders is trafficking in drugs?" Joy asked.

"That's a good possibility," Lawson said. "And I need all the information I can get. So please tell me everything, Terry."

"Okay," Terry said slowly. "Nica said she planned to put the drugs back in the room but someone moved everything out. She figured they would set it up again somewhere, so she waited until it was real late, then she went searching for the room. She found it set-up again next to the swimming pool."

"Do you have any idea who is taking part in this satanic worship?"

"No. Nica said the people at the meeting wore long black robes with hoods."

"You mean Nica actually saw one of the satanic worship meetings?" Lawson exclaimed.

"I'm not sure if she did or if she imagined she did," Terry said. "She told such a fantastic story that I can't believe it was really true."

"Maybe she was hallucinating from the drugs she used," Bob suggested.

"She said she didn't use any until after she saw the awful things at the meeting — but I think she did. Her story was too crazy to be real."

Although she remained silent, Joy's blue eyes mirrored her concern. An uneasy sense of danger danced on every nerve.

"Tell me what she said she saw," Lawson urged.

Terry swallowed hard. "She said a man sacrificed a-a little white dog and c-caught his blood. . . ."

"Did she say who the man was?" Lawson interrupted.

"No, she didn't see who any of the people were — because the hoods hid their faces."

"That is a fantastic story, all right," Lawson said. "Did she say anything else?"

"Yes, something more ridiculous, yet. Nica said she suddenly remembered that someone had tried to sacrifice her when she was a little girl, on the rock in the pool. Just where the little dog was killed."

Lawson shook his head sadly. "Nica was certainly hallucinating, all right. And I suppose she said her own father was the one who tried to sacrifice her."

"No, she didn't say who did. I don't really think she saw who did it. She got mad because I didn't believe her story and said she wouldn't tell me even if she did know who tried to kill her."

"It doesn't matter anyway," Lawson said. "The whole thing is too ridiculous for belief. Her father should be told so he can get help for her drug problem."

"Do you think her father is selling drugs?" Joy asked.

"I don't know, but we are going to find out," Bob said emphatically. He rose to go.

Terry sprang up and asked anxiously, "You're going to get us out of here, aren't you?"

"Before long," Lawson said quickly, "but for a while you are safer here. I. . . ."

Suddenly, the door swung open and Pascual entered with a paper sack. When he saw Lawson, he began to back out and stammered, "S-sorry, boss. I didn't know you were talkin' to the prisoners."

As Joy looked from one to the other, her incipient fear exploded. "Boss, Pascual? Do you work for Mr. Lawson?" she demanded of the flustered Mexican man.

Pascual stood in the doorway with a troubled expression on his swarthy face. His dark eyes darted to Lawson's face and he remained silent.

"You're one of the smugglers, aren't you?" Terry asked Lawson, aghast.

"What business do you have in here?" Lawson demanded of Pascual in an angry voice, ignoring the questions.

"I-I just brought some food for the-them. Even prisoners must eat, no?" Pascual said, lifting his eyebrows expressively.

"Leave it and get out!" Lawson said furiously.

Pascual dropped the paper sack on the floor and retreated rapidly out the door with a, "Sure, boss."

"*You* had us kidnapped!" Joy accused.

Lawson laughed unpleasantly. There was a triumphant gleam in his cold glare. "Yes, I'm the head of this operation, and you two have just told me everything I needed to know."

His arctic-green eyes went to Terry. "You did me a great service by your loyalty to Nica, by telling no one what you knew. Good boy!"

"Then will you let us go?"

"I'm afraid I can't do that. You know far too much," Lawson said. "It's regrettable that you two got involved, but I can't let you destroy what I have built up."

"You're going to kill us," Terry stated in a flat voice.

"After your usefulness is over, yes."

"My husband will be looking for us!" Joy said angrily. "You won't get away with this!"

"Oh, but I will," Lawson said softly. "Your husband has received a kidnapper's note so he has no idea you are back here. Later, another note will be delivered for him to pay money for you. But when you are found — back in the Tucson area, of course — you will be dead. The kidnappers panicked, did away with you, and fled."

"How are we still useful to you?" Terry demanded belligerently. His face was very pale but his blue eyes blazed with anger.

"I may let you attend one of my satanic meetings — as *very* special guests."

"Nica's story is true! Are you going to kill us like you did that poor little white dog? Sacrifice us?" Terry's voice broke on a hysterical note.

"Not a bad idea," Lawson said tauntingly. "Remember, you were the one who suggested it." He went out the door, chuckling sadistically.

"Perhaps he's just trying to scare us," Terry said, but his words lacked conviction.

"I think it is time we prayed again," Joy said. "You are old enough to know, Terry, that we're in deadly danger. Satan's unholy power is real. We have never needed God's help more desperately than we do now."

Taking Terry's cold hands in her own, Joy bowed her head and prayed aloud, for their safety, and for strength for Mitzie and Skye. "Father, you said that the name of Jesus is a strong tower. The righteous run into it and are safe. Terry and I are your children, and in the mighty name of Jesus, we ask your protection. You alone are stronger than Satan."

When she had finished, Terry asked falteringly, "Will God really set us free from these bad people?"

For a moment Joy looked at Terry, then said, "I believe He will, Terry, but we must be like the three Hebrew children in Daniel. They felt God could deliver them, but even if He didn't, they were still going to serve God as long as there was breath in their bodies."

"You think we are going to die," Terry said. His voice was flat.

Joy looked Terry directly in the eyes. "We prayed and I know God heard us. I believe He will someway set us free, but if He does not choose to — well, we will still be all right because we will just go to live with Him."

Terry looked troubled. "But doesn't . . . doesn't the Bible say something about God not forgiving us if we didn't forgive other people?"

Joy looked at him in surprise. "Are you having a problem with not forgiving someone, Terry?"

Terry dropped his eyes and walked over to the window. Joy followed him. "What is the problem, Terry? Tell me. Maybe I can help."

When he did not answer, Joy said gently, "Does it have to do with Mitzie?"

Terry's voice was low and miserable. "You wouldn't understand."

"Maybe I would. Give me a chance, Terry. Tell me what is bothering you."

"Y-you're her mother," Terry muttered, "you-you. . . ."

When he didn't go on, Joy probed gently, "Then it is Mitzie?"

"Don't you see?" Terry said roughly. "She's everybody's favorite. My father and I had just got to be friends, and then Mitzie had to come along! Then he liked her best!"

Joy started to protest but felt as if a stern warning finger were laid on her lips. At least Terry was talking to her! She mustn't blow it!

Terry swung around and faced her. His face was haggard and tense. "Nobody knows what it's like living in the same home as *perfect* Mitzie! She's pretty and I'm ugly. She's just the right size and I'm a runt! She knows how to make friends and has lots of them! I don't have any!"

Tears were running down his cheeks but Terry seemed unaware of them. "She's even smarter than I am! She makes good grades, and I never made a good grade in anything except reading and any dummy can read! I hate her, even if she is your daughter!"

Terry turned back to the window, rubbing the tears from his face with a trembling hand. "There! You wanted to know, so I told you!"

For a moment Joy did not know what to do or say. Then, her heart swelled with love, and she went to Terry, putting her arms about his slight form. At first, he stood stiff and unyielding in her arms.

She spoke softly. "Terry, why did you keep all of this bottled up? You are our son, and Skye and I love you very much. Why didn't you come to us and tell us how you felt?"

"I-I thought you wouldn't understand," Terry mumbled. "I thought you would h-hate me, if I didn't l-like Mitzie."

"We would never hate you, Terry! We love you!"

Terry drew back and searched Joy's face. She smiled, reached over, and touched soft lips to his forehead. "We do love you, Terry. You must believe that."

Suddenly Terry's face crumpled and he began to cry — deep, heart-wrenching sobs. Joy gathered him into her arms. For several minutes he sobbed like a small child. Joy held him close as she had done when he was younger and rocked him back and forth until his tears began to subside. A whisper of sound by the altar momentarily drew her eyes to the front of the room, but there was nothing there. She looked back down at Terry's head and held him close.

At last Terry drew away from her, mopping his wet face with his sleeve, and said self-consciously, "You-you must think I'm a-a baby."

Joy caught his face between her soft palms and kissed him gently. "You are my son and there is no age limit on that." She reached for Terry's hand and drew him over to two chairs. "Can we sit down and talk now — about the best way to handle your feelings for Mitzie?"

Terry sat down facing her, "I-I guess so."

"Do you really want to get rid of your resentment?" Joy asked. "You have to be completely honest with me — yourself — and the Lord."

Terry looked down at his hands and was thoughtful for a long moment. "I guess I have to get rid of it. If I don't tell God about it, He won't forgive me. And I sure need His forgiveness."

"Terry, first let me tell you something. Your father and I do not love you — or Mitzie — because of your good or bad points. We love you because you are our son and daughter. And we love you both exactly the same."

"But Mitzie's smarter and pretty. . . ."

"In the first place, Mitzie is not smarter.

She is just more interested in making good grades. It means more to her than to you." Joy leaned toward Terry and grinned. "And as for being better-looking, Mitzie told me that two of the girls from your school said they thought you were cute but that you seemed stuck-up."

A faint flush rose in Terry's face. "Honest — did they really say that?"

"Honest, they did!"

Joy's eyes twinkled. "I believe you have been so busy comparing yourself to Mitzie — and probably everyone else, too — that you've sold yourself short in everything. The secret to having friends is being friendly — and being yourself. Forget about yourself as much as possible. Relax and enjoy other people."

"I don't know how to talk to people, especially girls."

"Just show an interest in other people, make them feel good about themselves, and you *will* have friends. I can guarantee it," Joy said emphatically.

"I guess I never really tried to make friends much," Terry admitted.

"Now," Joy said, "let's ask the Lord to take away your resentment for your sister."

Joy saw a slight frown appear between Terry's eyebrows and said quickly, "The first step is admitting Mitzie *is* your sister." Joy smiled and said gently, "She is, you know, whether you admit it or not!"

"I-I guess so."

"I'm going to pray now, Terry, for God to remove the resentment from your heart. Then, I would like you to pray in your own words for God's help."

Joy prayed, simply and directly. Then she opened her eyes, smiled and said, "Your turn now."

Terry looked down at his hands. Joy could see that they were clenched and white. "I-I'm not sure I can."

Joy laid her hand on Terry's tense hands and spoke gently, "The best way I have ever found to overcome resentment is to pray for the person you resent."

"Mitzie doesn't need any help from the Lord," Terry said stubbornly. "She doesn't have any problems."

"What gave you that idea?" Joy asked. "Everyone has problems."

"What problems does *she* have?"

"You have been one," Joy said. "You will never know the number of times she has come to me crying when you hurt her feelings."

Terry was silent.

"And it has been a grief to her that her father was a criminal and died in a shootout with the police."

Terry's eyes opened wide. He had never heard this; he only knew that Mitzie's father was dead and that neither she nor Joy ever mentioned him. "What kind of criminal?"

"He was a jewel thief, an armed robber, and a very wicked and cruel man. Mitzie has always had the fear that she would inherit some of his bad character. I have prayed with her about it numbers of times."

"I didn't know," Terry said. "At least my mother was not — a — criminal, or bad." He was silent for a moment and then he looked at Joy with an intensely serious expression on his face.

"I think I see what my main problem is: I have always thought of myself and no one else. It's strange, but I never realized that other people had serious problems, too."

Joy watched several feelings cross his face, until suddenly, he seemed to make a decision. "I think I can pray now."

Joy could not keep the tears back as he prayed simply, "Heavenly Father, I'm sorry that I've only thought of myself for all these years. I'm sorry I've hated Mitzie. Forgive me, and help me to think of others.

"And, Father, help me to love my-my

sister. And help her with her problems, too. In Jesus' name I ask, Amen."

Joy looked at Terry, tears still misting her eyes. As he stood to his feet, his face held a look she had never seen there before: maturity? humbleness? strength? Maybe all three.

Terry leaned over and kissed Joy gently on the cheek, almost like a benediction. "Thank you, Mother. I love you."

25

Nica and her father were just finishing dinner when the telephone rang on a table nearby. Ruiz spoke briefly into the receiver, then brought the telephone to his employer. "It's Dr. Windthorn, sir," he said.

Richard's voice was warm as he spoke into the receiver, "Skye! How are you enjoying the sightseeing?"

Nica suddenly saw her father's body grow rigid as he exclaimed, "No! Joy and Terry kidnapped? When? How did it happen?"

He listened intently for a moment and then said slowly, "This is terrible, Skye. Have you heard from the kidnappers again?" He listened briefly and then said, "Where are you? Okay. I know where the Royal Hotel is. I'm coming in to be with you. I know the Sheriff. I'll go see him first. Maybe I can do something to help."

As her father hung up the phone, Nica stood up and asked incredulously, "Did someone kidnap Mrs. Windthorn and Terry?"

Richard looked at his daughter. "Yes. I'm going into Tucson. At least I can be moral support if nothing else. But, first, I must locate Bob Lawson and tell him about this development."

"Dad, there is something I have been trying to tell you all through dinner," Nica said slowly.

But her father was already moving toward the door. "Not right now. Another time, Nica," he said quickly. "I'm sure it can wait until I get back."

"But, Daddy," Nica said quickly, "this is important."

Her father turned back impatiently. "Make it fast then." He came back to stand at the table.

"D-did you know there is a satanic cult that meets here at our house?"

Richard chuckled mirthlessly. "There *were* satanic meetings going on here. I found the room and had the servants tear down the trappings. Then, I had a talk with all of the employees. I made it plain that I'll not tolerate any such rituals at The Boulders."

"But, Daddy, there was a satanic ritual at the pool — the night before the Windthorns left."

Richard stared at Nica incredulously, his face rigid. "How do you know?"

"Because I was there."

Richard's tone was grim. "After I warned them! I'll fire anyone who was present. Tell me who was there."

"They all wore black robes with hoods. I don't know who they were."

"What time was this meeting held?"

"Around midnight, I think," Nica said.

Richard's eyes narrowed. "What were you doing wandering around the house at that hour?"

"I found out the cult room had been moved so I was looking for it. I wanted to find it again so you would believe me when I told you about it. I had no way of knowing you were the one who tore it apart."

"It could have been dangerous intruding on a satanic ritual like that!"

"They didn't see me," Nica said, "but I would never go again; it was horrible! Daddy! They killed a little white dog as a sacrifice!"

"I swim at the pool nearly every morning, and I didn't see any blood or evidence of a satanic ritual," her father said slowly, his eyes narrowed in disbelief.

"T-they caught the b-blood and d-drank it," Nica said with a shudder.

Before her father could voice the horror she saw on his face, Nica rushed on, "As the priest drew back a long knife to k-kill the pitiful little dog, I suddenly had a memory flashback. I was almost killed by a satanic priest when I was real little — not more than three-years-old! He stood over me with a long knife, right over on the boulder where the little dog was killed!"

"Veronica! Talk sense," Richard demanded.

"It's true — whether you believe me or not!" Nica said defiantly.

Her father took a deep breath and let it out slowly. "Veronica, I'm trying to be patient. Now tell me the truth. You didn't really see a dog sacrificed on the boulder in the middle of our pool, did you?"

"Yes, I did!"

"Why did none of the servants — or me — hear or see anything?"

"Maybe the servants — and you, too — are all Satan worshipers," Nica said flippantly, angered that her father didn't believe her.

Richard's eyes sparked fire. "Don't be impudent, Veronica! I'm not forgetting the outlandish stories you told me when you were expelled from the exclusive schools we paid a lot of money to send you to: Let's see — you were physically abused by teachers; the math teacher wanted to elope with you, the. . . ."

"This is different," Nica said sullenly. "I really did see the satanic ritual. I. . . ."

"And I suppose you really did see a satanic priest standing over you with a knife," her father said scathingly.

"Yes, I did! But a woman screamed and he stopped," Nica said angrily.

A muscle jerked in Richard's jaw and his lips curled with contempt. "What do you take me for, Veronica? A complete fool? What is the purpose of this ridiculous story? To get attention? Well, it gets my attention all right, but not in a way that will help your case. Now go to your room and stay there until I return from Tucson!"

When Nica continued to stand and stare at him, Richard ordered sternly, "Go! Before I lose my temper and spank you like I should have long ago!"

Nica's slim, expressive face paled and tears rose in her green eyes as she jumped up from the table, almost colliding with Ruiz. She rushed out of the room and up the stairs to her room.

Once inside, she threw herself on her bed, fighting tears of anger, hurt, and frustration. Suddenly, a new thought rose in her mind, a horrifying thought that pushed aside her tears. It was the thought that had been trying to take hold in her mind ever since she had first found the satanic worship room — and the drugs there.

Maybe her father was involved in Satan worship! Worse yet, maybe he was a drug dealer! Her father was a wealthy man. With a sickening sensation in her stomach she asked herself: How could Satan worship — and perhaps drug dealing, too — go on in her father's mansion without his knowledge?

"Daddy would never do something like-like take part in satanic rituals — or deal in drugs," she said aloud. But he hadn't denied that he was a Satan worshiper when she had lashed out at him with that thoughtless accusation . . . or become upset at the evil it represented. He had only become angry and ordered her to her room.

A big lump formed in her stomach, and she clasped her hands over it to ease the cramps that suddenly gripped her. Was the kidnapping someway tied in with all of this? The Windthorns had brought in Luana. And Terry knew about the Satan worship room — and the drugs that came from there.

And that strange picture that had come so vividly into her mind. Was that a hallucination, a figment of an overactive imagination . . . or had it really happened?

A new idea made her sit upright on the bed. Her mother should know something about it — if it had really happened!

The spasms eased somewhat in her stomach. She tried to calm the racing of her heart before she picked up the telephone on her nightstand and dialed.

"Tucson Hospital of Hope," spoke a cool, professional voice in her ear.

"This is Veronica Borders. My mother is a patient in your hospital and I must talk to her."

There was a slight pause on the other end of the line and then the cool voice said crisply, "I'm sorry, that will not be possible. Only her husband is allowed to call her and then only briefly."

"It's an emergency. I have to talk with my mother!"

"I'm sorry. . . ."

"Let me talk to the head supervisor," Nica said in a voice that suddenly grew frigid and adult.

For a moment there was no sound and then the voice said stiffly, "I'm letting you speak with your mother. But if you upset her, you could cost me my job!"

"Thank you," Nica said sweetly.

In less than a minute Nica heard her mother's light, "Hello."

"Hello, Mother. Are you feeling better?"

"Nica! What a delightful surprise. Are you all right, dear?" Her mother's voice was warm and comforting against her ear.

"I'm fine," Nica said. "But-but. . . ."

"Is something wrong, Nica? Your father isn't sick — or something, is he?"

"Oh no, we are both fine. It's just that I needed to know something. You may think I'm making up stories, but. . . ."

"Yes, yes, what is it?"

Nica took a deep breath and then blurted out, "Mother, I wouldn't have disturbed you but this is extremely important. Did a satanic priest try to sacrifice me when I was a little girl?"

Nica heard a quick intake of breath on the other end of the line and then complete silence. "Mother! Are you still there?"

"Yes-yes, I-I'm still here, Veronica. Why-why do you ask such-such a question?" Her mother's voice was so faint she could scarcely hear it.

"Because I accidentally stumbled into a satanic ritual down at the pool in our house, and when-when the priest drew back his knife to k-kill the little white dog, I suddenly had a glimpse of myself in the same place as the dog."

Her voice rose a little. "I remembered that

238

I was lying on the boulder in the pool and a man in a black-hooded robe was standing over me with a long knife in his hand. Then I remembered that a woman screamed."

Her mother's voice sounded strained and unreal. "Who was the priest at the ritual you saw?"

"I don't know. His face was hidden by a black hood."

"Are there guests at The Boulders?"

"Bob Lawson is staying here part of the time, working on a smuggling case."

There was a clatter at the other end of the line.

"Mother, are you still there? Mother — Mother. . . ."

"Yes, dear, I-I just dropped the phone. Now, Nica, I want you to go to your father and tell him what you have told me."

"I already did, Mother, but he didn't believe me."

"Go get your father, Nica, I want to talk to him."

"He just left to go over to Tucson, to the Royal Hotel. The Windthorns, friends of father's who were here for a few days, went over to Tucson to do some sightseeing and someone kidnapped Mrs. Windthorn and their son, Terry. Daddy went over to try to help."

"Is — is Bob Lawson there now? I want to talk to him."

"I-I haven't seen him. I don't know if he is here right now," Nica said. Her heart was pounding. Something about her mother's voice was deeply disturbing. She sounded — terrified.

"Mother, you don't have to worry about me. The servants are here and our place is well guarded."

She heard her mother take a deep breath and could almost see her forcing calmness into her voice. Then she remembered her mother had not answered her original question.

"Mother, you never did answer my question about. . . ."

"Not now, baby. This is important. I want you to lock your door, and don't let anyone — not *anyone* — in. Do you hear me?"

Hot tears blurred Nica's eyes. Her mother hadn't called her "baby" for years.

"Why should I lock the door, Mother? Who should I be afraid of?" A shudder shook her slim frame. That she might be in danger had never entered her mind.

"Do as I. . . ." Her mother's voice was suddenly cut off and the line went dead.

Nica jiggled the phone button several times but no sound came from the instrument. With trembling fingers, she replaced the receiver and then lifted it again. There was no answering dial tone.

An icy chill slid down Nica's back, sending slivers of paralyzing fear shivering into every cell of her body. Mother thought she might be in danger! But from whom? Was someone crouching outside her door right now?

The thought galvanized her into action. Springing up, she dashed to the door and locked it. Then she darted to the windows and locked them securely. Creeping back to the door, she listened with her ear against the door. There was no sound anywhere out there.

"It's almost as if this huge old house is listening, too." Her voice sounded loud and echoing in the silence of her room and she shivered.

Nica did not undress and she did not plan to go to sleep but as the hours stretched out endlessly, she began to have to fight to stay awake. She couldn't keep her mind on a book she tried to read. And watching television was even worse. She found herself straining to hear strange sounds above the noise of the program.

After pacing about the room, doing exercises until her limbs and body were aching and eating all the little goodies she had stashed in her room, she finally plopped down on the bed to rest for a few minutes.

The next thing she knew, she awoke to a soft tapping at her door and darkness outside. Instantly wide awake, her heart pounded madly. At first she ignored the tapping, but when it continued, she finally got up and went to the door. "Who is it?"

"It's Bob Lawson," a voice said softly. "Please, let me in."

"M-my mother said to not let anyone in my room," Nica said.

"She didn't mean me, Nica," Lawson's voice said. "All the phone lines are dead, and I have reason to believe you may be in danger. I want to take you to a place of safety."

Nica was uneasy. The terror in her mother's voice had been real. "I'll be okay in here," she said. "Mother told me to stay here and not let anyone in," she reiterated.

"Nica, please believe me," Bob's voice said urgently, "you are not safe alone. I have just discovered that your house is being used for a multi-million dollar drug operation. Many of your servants are in on it. We don't know at this point who can be trusted or who can't. I could never face your father if I let anything happen to his daughter!"

Cold fingers of fear traced their way across her skin and Nica shivered. Had her mother known about the drug ring? Were her father and mother both involved in some way in this? A sob rose in her throat.

"Nica," Lawson's voice had an edge of impatience now, "I must go. If you choose to take your chances here alone, I guess there isn't anything else I can do. Either come right now or. . . ."

"I-I'm coming," Nica said. Suddenly, she could not bear another moment of solitude in this rambling, listening house. Swiftly she unlocked the door.

"Come quickly and don't make a sound," Lawson said curtly.

As Nica followed the long-legged stride of Bob Lawson down the hall, she heard soft footfalls behind them. Glancing back in sudden panic, she saw with relief that it was only Larry and Bill, Lawson's two aides. She relaxed. Who could harm her with three strong, capable men protecting her?

26

Joy lay quietly on the dirty mattress. Earlier that evening, Tiberio had come in and dumped the thin mattress on the floor, tossed a couple of flat, soiled pillows on top of it, and told them brusquely to go to sleep.

"And leave the night light on," he ordered, "so I can look in and see you without any trouble."

They had sat down on the mattress and talked in low tones. The black-draped walls gave the room an eerie feeling. But in spite of the desperation of their situation, Joy felt peace. Turning her head, she could barely make out Terry's face in the dim light. Love surged through her as she looked at his tousled blond hair and knew that his long struggle was over. "Thank you, Father, for this special son," she whispered.

Joy hadn't thought she'd fallen asleep, but a sudden noise at the door snapped her awake. Terry also sat upright. As they watched, footsteps shuffled to a stop and the door swung open. The overhead light was switched on. Blinking in the sudden glare, they saw Nica and Bob Lawson standing just inside the doorway. Beyond were Lawson's ever-present shadows, Larry and Bill.

Veronica gasped when she saw Terry and Joy. "Terry! Mrs. Windthorn! What are you doing here?" Before they could answer, she turned to Bob Lawson. "You didn't tell me you had found them. Have you called Daddy to let him and Dr. Windthorn know?"

Joy rose quickly to her feet and walked toward Nica. "Mr. Lawson did not find us, Nica," she said quietly. "He's the one who had us kidnapped and brought back here."

Nica's eyes widened in disbelief and she drew in her breath sharply. "That-that isn't true! It can't be! You wouldn't do such a thing, would you Mr. Lawson?"

Her green eyes swung in bewilderment to Lawson, back to Joy, and then back to her father's friend.

Joy saw a small, cruel smile curve Bob Lawson's lips. "I'm sorry, little Veronica, but I'm afraid their accusation is only too true."

"But . . . but . . . why?" Nica's voice edged the word with fear.

The faint grin vanished from Lawson's lips, and he answered with a cutting tone. "Your friend Terry knew too much and was too curious. Mrs. Windthorn just got caught in the trap when my men snared the runt here."

Joy could feel Terry stiffen, but he remained silent when Nica persisted, "But what did Terry know that would hurt you?"

"Oh, I'm not sure he could 'hurt' me. It's just that I don't believe in loose ends . . . especially in the mouths of children who can tell someone that there are drugs at The Boulders, or that satanic worship meetings are being held here."

"But . . . but I knew all of that! I'm the one who told him — and showed him!" Nica's face drained of all color as the last word left her mouth.

She faced Bob Lawson defiantly. "Am I a prisoner, too?"

When he only smiled his frosty sneer, she said faintly, "You're going to kill all of us . . . aren't you?"

Joy moved quickly to Nica's side and put her arm around her. "We are still alive," she said firmly. "And God is in control. He is stronger than this man and infinitely stronger than any power of Satan. He can keep us safe."

Lawson laughed, gloating and mocking. "And how is your God going to go about this deliverance? No one even knows where any of you are. Even if they did, we're in a hidden part of The Boulders. And all of you, except Nica, vanished many miles from here."

His harsh laugh grated on their ears. "And when you are found, you will all, again, be many miles from here."

His icy green eyes speared Nica. "Except for Nica. She will be found on the boulder in the middle of the pool, dead from an overdose of cocaine."

Nica's terrified eyes suddenly seemed to glaze and a moan of anguish came from her colorless lips. "You! You are the priest who-who killed the little dog, aren't you?"

Nica sagged against Joy and would have fallen if Terry had not jumped forward and supported her on the other side.

"The story Nica told me is true, isn't it?" Terry said angrily. "A man did try to kill her when she was a tiny little girl and that man was you!"

"Yes!" Lawson's face twisted with anger. "Monica, Veronica's mother, promised to give me her first child when it was born — to be used as a sacrifice — in return for a big favor. I fulfilled my part of the bargain, but she refused to give me her baby."

Nica's head snapped up. "How dare you lie about my mother! She would never promise to give her child to be sacrificed to-to-to. . . ."

Bob's cold eyes seemed to bore into Nica's and Joy felt her shudder. "My dear, ignorant child! If you knew the real truth about your mother, you could never lift up your head again!"

Suddenly Bob Lawson said brusquely, "Enough of this chit-chat! Suffice it to say that Monica stopped me. . . ."

"M-mother was the woman who screamed and kept you from murdering me!" Nica said.

"Yes — but not this time. She is far away in a hospital, and your father is in Tucson on his errand of mercy. Not that he ever suspected the truth!"

"W-what do you mean, 'not this time'?" Nica's query was only a whisper.

"You are all to be guests at a special ritual tonight," Lawson. "And you, my dear, are the chosen one — the sacrifice, as you were born to be!"

For a long moment Nica stared at Lawson with horror-filled eyes, then abruptly fell in a heap before Terry and Joy could prevent her. Shuddering sobs shook her frame. Joy gathered her into her arms and tried to comfort her, but she seemed not to notice. Her anguished moans seemed to fill the room.

Joy looked up as three figures were led into the room. She felt shock shudder through her.

Tiberio held two girls by the arms. Joy recognized Luana Torres, and the other had to be her sister, Conchita. A big burly Mexican with a curling mustache gripped a man who had his hands tied behind him. As they came in the man lifted his head, and Joy saw in amazement that it was Paul Tanner.

Even in the limited light of the room, Joy could see the lines of pain about Paul's tightly-pressed lips and the sweat beading his forehead.

"Look what you've done," Luana said angrily to Paul's captor. "You didn't have to be so rough; you've broken open his wound and it's bleeding again!"

Joy saw the red stain seeping through the bandage on Paul's shoulder. Her heart seemed to almost stop.

What was going on here? Was Paul the good guy? He must be if Bob Lawson was the bad — and he certainly was. Hope seemed to plunge to her toes, leaving a vacuum quickly filled with fear. But Joy moved swiftly across the room to Luana and no one stopped her.

When Luana saw her, her dark eyes brightened and she spoke excitedly in

Spanish. "*Señora* Windthorn, can you help us? *Señor* Lawson is the drug boss. He is going to kill us all!"

"I know," Joy said gently, taking the girl's hand in her own. "He kidnapped Terry and me, too. Is that your sister, Conchita?"

"*Si,*" Luana said. "Paul rescued us both, but I did not know he was our friend and I helped Lawson to capture us. They shot Paul when he tried to help us escape."

"How are you, Paul?" Joy asked.

"Not so great right now," Paul admitted.

"If only we could get you to a doctor. Is there anything I can do?"

"Get us all out of here," Paul said, with a slight grin.

"I can't do that — but God can," Joy said with sincerity. "Terry and I have prayed that He will do exactly that!"

Paul gazed at her for a long moment. "That is what my mother would say." For a moment he was thoughtful, then he said softly, "I have often wondered after some of my narrow escapes on the job if I would be alive if my mother had not prayed for me."

"You had better hope she is praying for you now! You're going to need it!" a taunting voice said. They turned to see Lawson standing nearby, a mocking, crooked grin on his face. "Do you all want to have a little prayer meeting right now and see if your God will hear you," he said with a mirthless chuckle.

"We are praying — even now," Joy said calmly. "God's in charge here — not you."

Glaring at her for a moment, Lawson's eyes narrowed, but he turned to Paul Tanner.

"I want to talk to you, Tanner," Lawson said in Spanish, seating himself in a chair and leaving his two big lieutenants near the door. "I would advise you to cooperate with me. If you don't, it won't go well with the two young ladies you have chosen to champion."

"I'll tell you everything you want to know if you'll let the others go," Paul said quickly.

"Wouldn't that be smart of me!" Lawson said. "Let them go to blab everything they know! Nice try, but I'm not stupid. I need the two *pollos* to frame you. You see," Lawson said derisively, "my men and I are going to have to shoot you out on the desert where you fled after you kidnapped the girls from us. Bullets from your gun will kill the girls, so it will naturally be assumed that you killed them because they were witnesses to your drug-running. We will even find some of the stuff on you!"

"And you think you can get away with that?"

"With my two men for witnesses, why not?"

Paul's eyes narrowed, but he remained silent.

Lawson chuckled maliciously. "But we do need a bit of information from you first."

"Why should I talk to you if you're going to kill us all anyway?"

"It would be a shame for that pretty little *Señorita* Conchita to go to her death with a carved-up face. And, of course, there's the totally unnecessary Mrs. Windthorn. If you do not cooperate, Detective Tanner, others will suffer — rather painfully — for your obstinacy."

Luana gasped. "Please, you wouldn't harm my sister!"

Conchita crowded close to Luana and Paul. She cowered next to Paul, clinging to his arm. "Please — don't let him hurt me!"

Bob laughed tauntingly. "Can you withstand that plea?"

"What do you want to know?" Paul said shortly.

"Just tell me how far your narcotic department's investigation has gone into my drug ring. What have you found out? Tell me every detail about your activities."

"I'm a very small duck in my department," Paul said. "I only know what I have done. I have circulated among the *coyotes* for some time and have become know as *La Vibora*. We have suspected — as you know — that drugs were being carried in by groups of Mexican illegals. We had not found out who was running the operation."

"Do you suspect Richard Borders?"

"We had no reason to suspect him until I trailed his men here with Conchita. He is now under surveillance, of course."

"By whom?"

"I have been watching his comings and goings and also those of his guests — through field glasses — since we got the girls away."

"Were the Windthorns under surveillance after they left here?"

"No, they were checked out when they first arrived and were obviously innocent of any involvement."

"Thank you, Detective Tanner," Lawson said. "Now, I want you all to make yourselves comfortable for awhile. Then you are my invited guests to a little religious ritual at midnight tonight. I hope you will find it enlightening."

He hesitated and then said as he walked to the door, "As a high priest in the Satanic Church, I have power to attain anything my heart desires. My high position in the government is but one example. You are helpless — and tonight," he paused, surveying each face as if to glean satisfaction from the paralyzed expressions, "tonight I will become more powerful."

Joy gripped Terry's hand tightly as Lawson said, "The satanic religion is a very old and respectable religion. And tonight's ritual will elevate me to a higher position in my satanic family. Tonight . . . I shall offer a sacrifice of blood."

"A blood sacrifice? You're crazy!" Paul exclaimed.

"You should have asked me whose blood," Lawson said softly. His green eyes burned with an intense light. "Until midnight, then, my friends." With a chilling laugh, he went out, followed by his aides.

27

Lawson looked at his watch and then at the little group of prisoners. "It is twelve o'clock. Our little band of worshipers seems to have been delayed. If they do not come in the next few minutes, we will proceed without them." His voice became harsh. "Nothing shall hinder me this time!"

"Please *Señor* Lawson, could you now untie Paul's hands? He is in much pain," Luana pled.

"No!" Lawson said emphatically. "I don't want him trying anything heroic."

"May I see if I can stop the bleeding of his wound, then? He is losing much blood!"

"Very well, but be quick about it," Bob said. "I want to start the ceremony as soon as the others get here."

"I will need bandages from the first aid kit," Luana said.

"Get them for her, Bill," Bob ordered, looking impatiently at his watch again.

As Bill went out, Lawson turned to the

others. "Come up to the front of the room where everything is prepared." He motioned with his hand, "Bring them, Larry."

Brandishing a gun, the silent Larry spoke only one word, "Move!" to the prisoners.

Nica moved forward with the others but she remained silent and listless. Lawson came to her and spoke almost gently. "It is really a great honor to be chosen as a sacrifice to the great one. Come, let me show you where you will lie."

"No!" She scrambled next to Joy and clung to her, her face hidden. Joy wrapped her arms about her protectively.

"Bring her to the altar," Lawson ordered Joy. When she hesitated, Lawson said, "Either move of your own accord, or I will have Larry — assist you."

Joy glanced at Nica and nodded. When they had walked the short distance to the altar, Lawson stepped up on the small raised platform which held the black-draped altar. Silently, he lighted the tall candles. Then, standing in front of the altar, he turned to face the others.

His silver hair glistened in the flickering candlelight and a small, crooked smile twisted his thin lips. His green eyes burned with an intense fire as he spoke.

"This altar is very old and has been

passed down to me from several generations of high priests."

He stepped from the platform and laid his hand upon Nica's shoulder and spoke as kindly as a father. "You do not need to fear, little one. I will give you a drug that will make you sleep, and you will never even know when the knife enters your heart."

"You didn't say anything about a knife," Terry said in a horrified voice. "You said Nica would be given an overdose of drugs."

"That I did," Lawson said lightly. "She will be dead from an overdose of drugs but with a knife in her heart."

Paul spoke for the first time, taking a step toward Lawson. "And how will you explain that?"

Luana edged in close behind Paul, her dark eyes peering from behind his shoulder were wide and intent upon Lawson.

"*I* will not have to explain anything," Bob said with a chuckle. "I won't even be around when she is found. But the knife will have Veronica's fingerprints on it; so naturally it will be presumed that she fulfilled that weird hallucination she had . . . and killed herself while high on cocaine."

"You are a monster," Joy said.

"Not really," Lawson replied. "I even regret that the child must die. But I must have a human blood sacrifice to please *my* god and to attain the higher position that only her blood can give me."

At that moment Bill came in with the first aid kit and moved toward them. Lawson took a step toward Bill. As he passed Paul, Paul moved with the swiftness of a desert rattler. He was suddenly behind the satanic priest, with one arm wrapped around his neck, the small knife Luana had slipped him after she slit his bonds, held to Lawson's throat.

"One move and I'll slit your throat," Paul said harshly.

The room froze into utter silence. Even Nica, huddled in Joy's arms, did not move or whimper.

Then Lawson moved so swiftly that later no one could tell how it happened; his hand flew up to clutch the hand that held the knife to his throat. At the same instant, his elbow flew back sharply to strike Paul in his wounded shoulder. Paul collapsed to the floor in agony.

Lawson stood over Paul's writhing body, a malicious smile on his cruel lips. "Even a well man would think twice before tackling Bob Lawson," he said mockingly. "And one with a clipped wing would never stand a chance."

He savagely kicked the wounded man in the head with the toe of his shoe, and Paul gasped with pain, trying to roll away from him. But Bob followed him and began to kick him viciously on the head and shoulders. Paul tried to protect his head and face by curling his chin down into his chest and covering his head with his arms.

Bob only laughed harshly and kicked him in the ribs. Before he could kick him again, though, Luana sprang over Paul and stood between his body and Lawson. "You are a wicked, evil man! Don't you touch him again!" she cried defiantly.

Lawson's cold eyes stared into Luana's flaming jet eyes for a full moment before he ordered harshly, "Larry, Bill, put these fools on the floor where they belong. And watch them! We're going to start the ceremony."

Lawson picked up the slim knife Paul had dropped and flipped it contemptuously into a dark corner of the room.

Then he reached over and wrenched Nica from Joy's arms.

Terry flew at him, trying to tear Bob's hands from her arms, pounding him with his balled fists. But the powerful man just seemed to flick his wrist, and Terry was tossed into the air like a rag doll. He landed, gasping for breath, on the floor. Joy ran to him and held him as Luana sat on the floor beside Paul and Conchita.

Lawson lifted Nica easily and stepped toward the altar — then froze. A figure rose from behind it like a wraith. The satanic priest jumped back, then stood as if turned to granite.

The figure was dressed in a pure white robe with gold trim edging the neck and sleeves. Long, pale, honey-brown hair was drawn back from a delicate, almost transparently-white face by a gold band. Slanted, brilliant eyes of deep emerald green stared from between long, dark lashes.

"Mother!" Nica let out the strangled cry and struggled to free herself.

But Bob tightened his hold, drew himself up regally, and spoke sharply. "Stand aside, Monica. This is a sacrifice to the great one . . . you have no part in it."

"A blood sacrifice?" The husky voice was soft but it seemed to penetrate every nook and cranny of the room.

"Yes! Now stand aside and let me get on with it," Lawson ordered hoarsely.

"Are you afraid I will interfere — like I did eleven years ago, Bob, when you tried to murder my only daughter?"

"There's nothing you can do this time, Monica! Now stand aside, before I. . . ."

"Before you kill me, too? Your baby sister? Have you no conscience, Bob Lawson? You tried once to kill your little niece. You would have drunk the blood from her tiny little body to appease the lust of your god who is only a god of sin and darkness and evil. Now you are trying to murder my child again! But you shall not!"

"Get her out of here, Larry!" Bob shouted hoarsely. "I'll deal with her later. No one is going to spoil this moment for me!"

"What about me, Bob?" a commanding voice spoke from the doorway.

Startled, Bob, his two henchmen, and the prisoners, turned to see Richard Borders standing just inside the door. Along the back wall, the sheriff, his deputies, police-men, and detectives stood with guns drawn and ready.

Bob Lawson's face went ashy-white. Like a cornered rat, his eyes darted desperately about the room, searching for a way out. Then, like a big, lithe cat, he sprang toward Monica, but she snatched up the long, shining knife that lay on the altar.

"Just try to lay a hand on me, Bob Law-son," she said shrilly. "Killing is too good for one who has preyed on the innocent of the world as you have! Growing rich from drugs while destroying the lives of those who buy them . . . enticing young and restless youth into your hellish satanic cult."

Her delicate face twisted with repugnance. "Think about the hell you have created for those who have become addicted to drugs through your trafficking! Addicts who prey upon old people and children to feed the demons you have unleashed inside them. It would be a public service to kill you like the mad dog you are!"

Bob Lawson's face turned a sickly yellowish-green as Monica, her emerald eyes glittering, stepped toward him with the knife drawn back menacingly.

"No, Monica," Richard Borders called urgently as he walked quickly toward her. "Give the knife to me. Let the law punish this man."

"But will they?" Monica looked up at her husband with anguished eyes as she surrendered the knife. "If I thought he would get off scot-free like so many do, I think I would kill him myself."

"With all the evidence you have gathered, I don't think you need worry about that, Mrs. Borders," the sheriff said, moving up to snap handcuffs on Bob Lawson.

Monica's laugh was a little shrill as she stooped and brought a small cassette recorder from underneath the black drapings of the altar. "I hid under your devilish altar before you arrived, Bob, and recorded every word you have spoken."

She handed it to the sheriff who said with grim satisfaction, "You are a brave lady, Mrs. Borders. With this as evidence and the testimonies of all the witnesses in this room, I think this drug king will be a very old man before he gets out of prison — if he ever does!"

28

Ringed by detectives and policemen with drawn weapons, three deputies searched Lawson and his two aides. At the sheriff's order, they not only handcuffed them but shackled their feet as well.

"I'm taking no chances with these prisoners," Sheriff Gomez said grimly.

Only then did Monica move around the altar and hold out her arms. "Come here, baby," she said softly to Nica.

Nica ran to her mother and clung, sobbing like a small child. Richard put his arms around both his wife and daughter and held them close.

After a few minutes, Veronica drew away from the circle of her parents' arms and asked shakily, "H-how did you know where we were?"

"Your mother is the real heroine here," her father said huskily. "And I'm the fool. I'm so sorry, Nica, that I didn't believe your story."

"I don't blame you, Daddy. It was so far

out I wasn't sure it was true either — the memory flashback, I mean." She turned to her mother. "You didn't tell me how you knew where we were."

"It's a long story, and I'll tell you all of it soon but when you told me my brother was here — and Bob is my brother — and the strange things that were going on, I was terribly afraid for you. Then, when the phone went dead, I knew you were in real, immediate danger. So I called the sheriff — your father had just arrived at his office — and we came as fast as we could get here."

Richard Borders said bitterly, "If you hadn't called your mother, you might all be dead by now. I'll never forgive myself! My stupidity nearly cost all of you your lives."

"You can't blame yourself," Monica said gently. "The story about Bob trying to kill her would be hard to believe."

"I didn't believe her either when she told me," Terry said from near them. "If I had gone to my father with the story, though, it might have saved all of us a lot of problems."

"I doubt it," Richard said. "Your father would have come to me, and I still would not have believed Nica's story."

"I'm so thankful you are impulsive, Nica," Monica said, hugging her." If you had not decided to call me, I'm afraid. . . ." She left the sentence dangling.

"And I have reason to believe he was planning to frame me and let me take his fall as drug lord," Richard said. "What a fool I have been in blindly trusting that man!"

Unable to understand the English conversation, but knowing they were safe now, Luana moved over to sit beside Paul on the floor. Removing his blood-soaked shirt, she tried to use it as a bandage, but the wound was bleeding badly. Dark red bruises discolored his face and body.

The sounds of sirens in the courtyard caught her attention briefly, and a few moments later, paramedics hurried into the room.

Nodding at them, Luana moved back as they took over and began to work on Paul's wound, trying to staunch the flow of blood.

Paul's face twisted with agony. One of his eyes was almost swollen shut and blood trickled down the side of his face from a gash above his eye.

Suddenly, Paul's eyes, dark with pain, opened and fixed on Luana.

"I'm sorry you are in so much pain," she said softly.

His left hand came up slowly and wiped the tears from her cheeks. His battered lips moved, and she bent to hear his words.

"It isn't so bad to hurt. Thank God, we are alive," he whispered.

"Yes, *Señora* Windthorn's prayer was answered," Luana said.

"*Si,*" Paul whispered earnestly. "I think I must find out more about Jesus Christ when this is over."

"That is my desire as well," Luana said softly.

Suddenly Conchita appeared and knelt down by Paul's head. She bent over him and smoothed his hair back with a shapely, soft hand. "They are bringing the stretcher for you," she purred. "Just lie very still and let me stroke your head until they come."

Swift anger rose in Luana like a black storm as Paul closed his eyes with a sigh.

Luana jumped up and nearly collided with a paramedic. "I'm sorry," she murmured in Spanish as she backed out of his way.

"Could you please move back so we can work on this man?" one of the paramedics directed Conchita, still at his side. She stepped away, and two other men knelt beside Paul.

As Terry, Joy and the Borders gathered near Conchita to watch, Luana moved back behind them, but the sheriff came up and spoke to Luana in Spanish. She saw that he was Hispanic and so were two of his deputies. Leading her to a chair, he began to question her about their ordeal. A sandy-haired young man with blue eyes, fair hair, and a sunburned nose — but who seemed to speak fluent Spanish — took notes as she shyly tried to answer the questions.

Suddenly, one of the detectives came up and whispered something to the sheriff.

Sheriff Gomez's dark eyes twinkled, and he turned back to Luana. "This is interesting. Detective Paul Tanner, a confirmed bachelor who has managed to elude all matrimony-minded females, at last has a girl."

"He does?" Luana said, misery plain in her voice.

"You don't even admit it? Maybe that's the secret," Sheriff Gomez chuckled. "Play hard to get."

Luana dropped her head in confusion as the sheriff continued, "Detective Tanner is insisting that his girl be allowed to go with him in the ambulance."

"I-I'll get Conchita," Luana mumbled. Her heart felt like it was being twisted and wrung out by a giant hand as she walked back to Conchita who was watching deputies and detectives lead Lawson and his two aides away to a police car.

Luana tried to speak once and her voice came out squeaky. She stopped, steadied herself and said quickly, "The sheriff said Paul wants you to ride in the ambulance with him."

Conchita stood silent for a moment and then said tartly, "No, he doesn't! Paul wants *you* to go with him. I heard him myself! And after I have wasted my time being nice to him!" Turning away she said angrily, "Go on and go with him! See if I care!"

Luana watched her flounce off, her mouth open in amazement. Her heart did a couple of flip-flops, and then began to pound like it was trapped inside her ribcage and was trying to escape.

Still not convinced that Paul had really asked for her, Luana slipped into the circle of people around Paul and moved to where she could see his face. His eyes were closed and one of the paramedics was attaching a bottle of something to Paul's arm.

He looked very pale under his bronze tan. A heavy bandage covered the wound on his chest. His left eye had puffed out and was now red and black. His lips were also bruised and swollen. Her heart leaped in anguish for him. How he must hurt!

"Luana."

Luana looked up and saw Paul looking at

her with a strange, penetrating gaze from the eye that wasn't swollen shut.

He slowly reached out his hand to her, and she ran to him and slipped her hand in his. It closed on hers, warm and strong, even in his weakened condition.

He drew her closer to him and whispered weakly, "Luana, please come with me to the hospital. I-I need you."

"Time to go, Paul," one of the paramedics said.

Paul ignored the paramedic. "The pain killer is taking effect, and I can't seem to stay awake," he said laboriously. "Promise me you will stay with me."

"I promise."

Slowly Paul raised Luana's hand and touched his bruised lips to her palm. "Did I ever tell you what lovely eyes you have?" he said softly. His dark eye, looking deep into hers, was warm and caressing.

Before she could answer, his eye closed and his breathing became deep and steady.

Glancing up, Luana realized that everyone was watching their every move and hearing their every word but, suddenly, she didn't care.

29

The spacious entry room of The Boulders was ablaze with lights even though it was after four o'clock in the morning. Richard and Monica came across the glistening tile floor to welcome Skye and Mitzie with outstretched hands.

"The children and Joy are asleep," Monica told them, "but they wanted to be right here when you arrived so the kids are bedded down in sleeping bags over there under the subdued light near the palm tree, and Joy's on the couch."

"Are they okay? I know you said they were, but it is almost too good to believe that we've got them back safe and well," Skye said huskily.

"Terry has a few bruises from being thrown to the floor by my brother-in-law, but otherwise they are both fine," Richard said. "You should be really proud of that boy, Skye. Joy said he flew into Bob like a tiger when he tried to harm my daughter."

"He really did, Skye," Joy said, coming

271

swiftly across the floor. Skye ran to meet her and picked her up from the floor in his long arms and kissed her soundly. When he set her down, Joy clasped Mitzie to her. Both were laughing and crying at the same time.

Awakened by the noise, Terry came almost hesitantly to his father. Skye caught him in a bear hug and Terry clung to his father fiercely.

"Now," Skye said, wiping tears from his eyes. "What is this I hear about you defending Nica like a real hero?"

Terry averted his eyes and flushed. "I-I tried to keep Mr. Lawson from hurting Nica, but-but I'm afraid I didn't do so well."

"You tried and that's what counts," Nica's mother declared firmly.

"Paul would have rescued us if he hadn't been so weak from being shot," Terry mumbled.

"So Paul Tanner is really an undercover narcotics agent?" Skye said, addressing Richard.

"And so is one of our maids," Monica added. "Margie helped Paul take Luana from The Boulders and also gave him the layout of our house so he could rescue Conchita."

"Let's all sit down so we can talk," Richard said. "There are refreshments here."

"All of our servants except Margie, the narcotics agent, are in jail," Monica said as they seated themselves. "They all worked for Bob Lawson and were part of his cult, also. Bob wondered why they didn't come to the ritual he had planned last night, but they were all arrested as soon as the sheriff got here."

Richard laughed. "Monica and I drove up to the guardhouse, and I jumped out and caught the guard before he could call the house and alert Bob. The sheriff's men systematically arrested the whole lot as soon as I let his men into the house."

"I knew about the secret part of the house, so I slipped in and set up a recorder while the sheriff was finishing up here," Monica continued. "We needed all the evidence we could get against Bob and his ring. There's a secret entrance under the altar so I hid there and waited. It was really hard to stay put when I heard you crying, Nica," Monica said, hugging her daughter to her, "but I needed to get everything I could on the tape before I revealed my presence. I couldn't even let Joy and Terry know I was there."

"The sheriff called a little while ago and said some of Bob's men have already started talking. A few of them had been wanting to get out of the drug racket and the cult, too, but they were deathly afraid of Bob."

"Were any drugs found?"

"Several million dollars' worth, stored in that secret storage place where they held us all captive," Joy said. "The sheriff said it was brought in all kinds of ways, illegal aliens crossing over, small aircraft, hidden in secret compartments of vehicles crossing the border into the States."

"Once in awhile a load was caught, but Bob had always been careful that nothing could be traced to him . . . until this time," Richard said.

"How did Bob ever get involved in drugs and a satanic cult?" Joy asked Monica.

"If you aren't too tired, I'll tell you the whole story," Monica said.

"We want to hear every word," Skye said emphatically. "I was really concerned when Richard didn't arrive at the hotel."

Monica passed more cookies and tea around, and urged everyone to make themselves comfortable. Then she sat down next to her husband.

"It is almost beyond my imagination even yet that Bob is a drug lord," Richard began. "I would have trusted Bob with my very life. And Nica and I learned for the first time tonight that he is my wife's brother."

Monica's green eyes glistened with tears. "It's a long, terribly sad, and bizarre story," she said gravely, wiping her eyes.

She laid her long slim fingers on her husband's arm. "If I had only had the courage to tell Richard the truth long ago, untold sorrow and misery could have been avoided for our own family as well as the many other lives that Bob has helped to ruin.

"But I was afraid that I would lose Richard, and my soft, easy life. Also, I was terrified of Bob. He's an evil man and always has been! A fearsome, frightening man who bullied me as a child and continued to do so up until the present."

"We would like to hear about it, if it isn't too painful," Skye said earnestly.

"I want to tell it," Monica said. "I don't want to have any more secrets from anyone.

"Our family was poor when I was a child," Monica began. "Bob was fifteen years older than I was, and there were five children between us. Father abused us children. Mother was terrified of him, too, and never interfered, no matter what he did to us. And Bob knocked us kids around even worse."

"Was your family part of a satanic cult, too?" asked Joy.

"Yes. I understand that my family brought

their evil religion with them when they migrated from England several generations ago. Not all were practitioners, but many of them were."

Monica dropped her eyes in shame. "My-my father forced me into prostitution when I was a child — as part of the satanic worship. I had to do as I was told, but I was never a Satan worshiper."

"You don't have to tell us about this," Skye said. "It must be very painful for you."

"I never want to hold anything back again," Monica said vehemently. "I would rather the whole world knew my life like a book than to go on hiding the truth.

"To make a living, my father sold drugs to the other members of his satanic brotherhood — they are used in the rituals, you know. He should have had lots of money, but he became an addict and most of his money went to satisfy his own habit. He died when I was ten from some bad drugs he used.

"Then Bob moved into his slot as head of the family and became the leader of the satanic church in our area. After that, he rose rapidly in the world of business. Bob has a magnetic personality and is cunning and smart. He made influential friends in high places and was appointed to positions of trust.

"The ones he couldn't sway with personality, Bob put under obligation to him, or under fear, in some cases."

Monica's voice grew bitter. "Bob soon lived in a fine house but he wouldn't help any of his family unless it was to his advantage. My mother and I still lived in a rat-infested apartment in a ghetto."

"Monica was only fifteen — although I thought she was eighteen — when I met her," Richard interjected.

Monica gulped back a sob, and Richard reached over and put his arm around her tenderly.

"Bob promised he would do all he could to promote a marriage between Richard and me, if I would promise to-to. . . ." Monica broke down and began to cry, heartrending sobs of bitter grief.

"She had to promise to give her brother our firstborn child as a sacrifice to Satan," Richard finished grimly. "I never knew about any of this until Monica told me coming home last night."

"But you didn't keep your promise," Joy said in empathy.

"No, when the time came, of course I couldn't. But at the time Bob approached me, I would have promised anything to escape the horror and shame of the life I was living at home. Bob fitted me out with a few beautiful clothes, a new hair-do and contrived a meeting for me with Richard.

"I was instantly enthralled with Richard. He was handsome, a gentleman, and very wealthy. And wonder of wonders, Richard fell in love with me! We were married after only a few weeks of whirlwind courtship.

"I was deliriously happy," Monica said as she laid her head on Richard's shoulder, "and I tried to avoid seeing my brother ever again. I didn't even invite him to our wedding. And I didn't — see him — for two years. Bob didn't seek me out and I tried to forget him . . . but sometimes it took alcohol and lots of it to forget the horrible promise I had made to him.

"I was very careful not to get pregnant. But — but something went wrong and it happened — after two years. I tried to convince myself that Bob would not try to make me keep a promise I had made under duress. But, unless my brain was fogged with alcohol, I knew he would."

"You mean he actually demanded your baby when Nica was born?" Skye interposed.

"He waited until I was home from the hospital with my beautiful little daughter before he put in an appearance," Monica said. "I had begun to hope that Bob wasn't going to come at all, when he didn't show up for a month. Then Richard was away on business and Bob came — late at night. He just appeared in my room."

"Did you live here then?" Joy asked.

"Yes, and I wondered how Richard had gotten in so easily. At that time I didn't know that all the guards around this house were in his employ."

"And still were — until tonight," Richard said. "Bob had set the stage for me to buy this house — with the secret courtyard and storage rooms that he and his drug-running partner had built into it. I was such a fool. I'd always liked unusual architecture. The house was bait Bob knew I couldn't resist. His partner sold it to me, and they continued to run their drug business from here. The guards, the servants — I thought I hired them, but they were really their henchmen, part of the drug gang . . . and the satanic cult."

"Does he still have a partner?" Skye asked.

"No," Monica said. "The man met with an accident shortly after Richard bought this house from him. I'm sure he was no longer useful to my brother, so Bob arranged his death. But I couldn't prove that."

"You were telling about your brother coming for the baby," Joy reminded her. "What did you do?"

"He demanded that I give my little Veronica to him. He said he would make it appear like a kidnapping, and the baby would just disappear. I flatly refused. He threatened to tell Richard about my life as a prostitute."

Monica's eyes suddenly twinkled. "But for once I used the brains I was born with! Some damaging evidence against my brother had accidentally come into my possession. I told him about it and that I had instructed a lawyer to turn it over to the police if anything happened to me.

"He was furious, but for once I stood my ground. The life of my child depended upon it. Bob agreed to a truce. I could keep the child if I would not turn the evidence over to the police. But I knew from the look in his eyes, and what I knew of my brother, that he would never give up that easily."

"Bob Lawson — as my friend," interposed Richard, "would show up once in a while for a visit, and I thought it strange that Monica always said she was sick and stayed in her room until he left."

"I lived in perpetual fear," Monica continued. "When Veronica was three, Richard had to be away for a month. I drank almost constantly. I was terrified of what my brother might try while he was away."

"What happened?" Joy asked breathlessly.

"One of the servants — at Bob's order, I'm sure — must have tried to drug my drink one night. But I had suddenly decided that night — after I had sipped a little of my cocktail — that I was going to quit drinking. I did that periodically because I was afraid I was becoming addicted. So I poured the drink out after sipping only a little of it and went to bed.

"When I woke up, I had a terrible, uncanny feeling that Veronica was in trouble. I ran to her nursery next door and she was gone. I was frantic, not knowing where in this monstrous house she might be. I was afraid to trust any of the servants.

"Then I recalled Bob saying that when his friend, who was also a Satan worshiper, had owned this house, they had had a satanic ritual at the pool. So I ran through the house barefooted, putting on my robe as I ran.

"When I burst through the glass doors into the pool area, I saw Bob, robed in black, with a knife drawn over my baby. I went berserk, screaming like a demented woman. I raced across the little bridge that had been laid over to the rock in the middle of the pool and snatched my child off the make-shift altar."

"What did Bob do?" Joy asked.

"I think for once he was too rattled to do anything. I was like a wild thing, screaming and babbling hysterically and all but foaming at the mouth. I guess I was pretty scary.

"Anyway, Bob made me a promise then that he would never try to harm the child again if we could make a covenant. I promised not to tell anyone about any of his activities, and he would release me from my promise and not tell Richard of my shameful life."

"It will always haunt me that I didn't believe Veronica when she told me about remembering that horrible ritual when her uncle tried to kill her," Richard lamented.

"It's really my fault," Monica said sadly. "If I hadn't been afraid to tell you the truth, Bob would have been in prison long ago. But instead of facing up to my responsibility, whatever the consequences, I tried to hide in a bottle of alcohol."

"But you did the right thing at last," Joy said gently. "That's what counts. And we're all alive because of it."

"Daddy and I were scared to death when you and Terry disappeared," Mitzie told her mother, "but we prayed, really hard."

"So did we," Terry spoke up. "And God answered all of our prayers."

Mitzie grinned at him. For a second Terry met her gaze steadily, then he grinned companionably.

Joy and Skye caught the new camaraderie and their eyes met over the heads of their children and held, speaking volumes.

"You've told us in bits and pieces about what happened last night, but I would like to hear the whole story," Skye said. "Why don't each of you tell your part of what happened."

After the stories were told, Monica said gently, "At the rehabilitation hospital this time I have been faithfully attending the AA meetings and chapel. I've begun to believe that God has the answer to my problems. After tonight, I'm convinced He does."

Terry spoke shyly. "I got some things worked out with the Lord, too, through all of this."

"I'm glad," Skye said. He reached over and pulled Terry up close, his grey eyes warm and misty as they rested on his son.

"Is Paul going to be all right?" Skye asked Richard.

"I called the hospital, and they said the bullet has been removed and he is resting. He should recover completely. Sheriff Gomez says he's a really good detective."

"Another exciting thing happened, too," Nica said. "I think Paul and Luana are in love."

"Well, tell me about this," Skye asked.

"You ought to have seen Luana when Paul asked her to go to the hospital with him," Nica said. "She was almost as pretty as Conchita with her dark eyes all shiny and her face just glowing."

"Girls! Always interested in romance," Terry said, rolling his eyes.

"Give yourself a few more short years, and you'll like it, too," his father laughed, rumpling his hair.

"By the way, where is Conchita?" Joy asked.

"The sheriff took her to Paul's mother," Richard said. "I understand that Luana and Conchita will be staying with her, under heavy guard, until after Lawson's trial. By that time I expect ways will be found for them to stay in the States. We'll do what we can."

"Richard and I were talking about it while we waited for you," Monica said. "We're going to visit the girls and encourage them to learn English. After the trial, we will pay for their education, if they want to go to school."

"And we're hoping you will come back to

The Boulders now that the danger is past, Skye," Richard said softly. "Monica and I want to learn more about the Lord, and I think you could help us tremendously."

He looked down at Nica and said gently, "I could also use a little coaching in being a real father. Monica and I don't plan to send our lovely little girl away to boarding school again. She's growing up fast, and we want to redeem what time we have left by having her home."

Veronica jumped up and threw her arms around first her father and then her mother. Tears sparkled in her eyes as she said shakily, "We'll be a real family!"

Skye and Joy looked at the smiling faces of their children, then at each other. The look Skye gave her was as warm as a hug.

"So will we," Joy whispered, "so will we."

The employees of Thorndike Press hope you have enjoyed this Large Print book. All our Thorndike and Wheeler Large Print titles are designed for easy reading, and all our books are made to last. Other Thorndike Press Large Print books are available at your library, through selected bookstores, or directly from us.

For information about titles, please call:

(800) 223-1244

or visit our Web site at:

www.gale.com/thorndike
www.gale.com/wheeler

To share your comments, please write:

Publisher
Thorndike Press
295 Kennedy Memorial Drive
Waterville, ME 04901